THE DEFINITIVE ARIZONA BUCKET LIST

GUIDE BOOK

Over 110 Incredible Journeys and Exploration Spots to Turn Your
Travel Aspirations into Unforgettable Memories!

+ Arizona Map & Journal Log Section

Michael Kendall

Credits

set_8610451.htm#query=usa%20license%20plate&position=12&fro
m_view=keyword&track=ais
    License type: Free License/Public Domain
    Author: Image by pch.vector on Freepik
17. Cover Image: https://www.shutterstock.com/image-photo/road-
    monument-valley-during-sunny-day-1898007784
    License Details: Roaylty-free

TABLE OF CONTENTS

About Arizona 12

The Map of Arizona.. 15

Why Visit Arizona?... 16

How To Use The Book 17

AJO.. 18

    Cabeza Prieta National Wildlife Refuge 18
    Organ Pipe Cactus National Monument 19

APACHE JUNCTION 21

    Goldfield Ghost Town 21
    Lost Dutchman State Park.. 22

BENSON 23

    Kartchner Cavern State Park.. 23
    Quarles Art 24

BISBEE 25

    Center Town Old Bisbee, Arizona 25
    Lavender Pit.. 25
    Muheim Heritage House 26
    Mule Pass Tunnel.. 27

BOUSE 28

    East Cactus Plain Wilderness.. 28

CAMP VERDE.. 29

    Fort Verde State Historic Park 29
    Montezuma Castle National Monument 30

CHINLE 31

    Canyon De Chelly National Monument.. 31
    Hope Arch.. 31

CIBECUE 33

    Cibecue Creek 33

CLARKDALE **34**

Arizona Copper Art Museum... 34
Verde River Access.. 34

FLAGSTAFF **36**

Buffalo Park... 36
Cococino Lava River Cave 37
Downtown Flagstaff... 37
Frances Short Pond 38
Fort Tuthill County Park 39
Lowell Observatory.. 40
Riordan Mansion State Historic Park............................. 40
Sunset Crater Volcano National Monument 41
Walnut Canyon National Monument 41
Wupatki National Monument.. 42

GANADO **44**

Ganado Lake 44

GILBERT **45**

Freestone District Park.. 45
Riparian Preserve At Water Ranch 45
Water Tower Plaza.. 46

GLOBE **47**

Besh-Ba-Gowah Museum 47

HOLBROOK.. **48**

Rainbow Forest Museum 48

JEROME **49**

Audrey Headframe Park... 49
Jerome State Historic Park.. 49

KAYENTA... **51**

Navajo Shadehouse Museum 51

LAKE HAVASU CITY **52**

London Bridge 52

NOGALES **53**

Patagonia Lake State Park.. 53
Nogales Border Plaza.. 54

PAGE **55**

Antelope Canyon... 55
Carl Hayden Visitor Center... 55
Horseshoe Bend 56
Lake Powell 57
Water Holes Canyon 57

PEACH SPRINGS **59**

Grand Canyon Caverns 59
Hualapai River Runners.. 59

PHOENIX **61**

Arizona Science Center.. 61
Camelback Mountain 62
Cave Buttes Recreation Area 62
Civic Space Park 63
Desert Botanical Garden 64
Encanto Park 64
Heard Museum... 65
Heritage And Science Park 65
Hole In The Rock... 66
Phoenix Bat Cave.. 67
Phoenix Zoo 68
South Mountain Park And Preserve................................. 68
The Duce 69

PINE **70**

Fossil Creek Dam.. 70
Native American Ruins.. 70

PRESCOTT **72**

Courthouse Plaza... 72
Watson Lake Park 72

SCOTTSDALE... **74**

Arizona Boardwalk 74
Butterfly Wonderland 74
Chaparral Park... 75
Frank Lloyd Wright Spire 76

Huhugam Ki Museum 77
Macdonal's Ranch 77
Mccormick-Stillman Railroad Park 78
Mcdowell Sonoran Preserve 79
Octane Raceway 79
Odysea Aquarium 80
Old Town Scottsdale 81
Pinnacle Peak Park 81
Scottsdale Museum Of Contemporary Art 82
Scottsdale Xeriscape Garden 83
Sereno Park 83
Soleri Bridge 84
Sunrise Peak 85
Taliesin West 86
Wonderspaces Arizona 86

SEDONA **88**

Amitabha Stupa And Peace Park 88
Bell Rock 88
Slide Rock State Park 89
Chapel Of The Holy Cross 90
Red Rock State Park 90
Sedona Performing Arts Center 91
Snoopy Rock 92
Tlaquepaque Arts And Crafts Village 93
Rio Salado Habitat 93

TEMPE **95**

Legoland Discovery Center Arizona 95
Lopiano Bosque Habitat 95
Rio Salado Park 96
Tempe Beach Park 97

TUCSON **98**

Arizona-Sonora Desert Museum 98
Catalina State Park 98
El Presidio Historic Distric 99
Fort Lowell Park 100
International Wildlife Museum 100
Mission San Xavier Del Bac 101
Prima Air & Space Museum 102
Reid Park Zoo 103

Trail Dust Town 103
Tucson Botanical Gardens 104
Tumamoc Hill 104

TOMBSTONE **106**

Bird Cage Theater 106
O.k. Corral 106

TUSAYAN **108**

Grand Canyon National Park 108

WINSLOW **110**

Meteor Crater Natural Landmark 110

Arizona Itineraries And Trips Proposals **111**

Absolutely loved your Arizona Bucket List Guide? **121**

About Arizona

(1)

This rugged western state is a place of extremes, from the world's largest stand of towering evergreen ponderosa pines to sun-scorched deserts dotted with prickly pear cacti and creosote bushes. Parts of Arizona are known for expansive, arid desert landscapes, but the state actually boasts tons of shoreline thanks to its many large, artificial lakes like Lake Powell and Lake Mead formed by damming the Colorado River.

From 1850 to 1912, Arizona was part of New Mexico Territory before finally earning statehood on February 14, 1912 as the 48th state. In those early territorial days, waves of Anglo-American settlers and entrepreneurs poured in, hoping to strike it rich in the burgeoning mining industry, while most Hispanic folks stuck around in New Mexico instead of venturing northwest. The climate and terrain tended to attract more rugged, adventurous pioneer types willing to brave the harsh, arid landscape.

Up until 1940, Arizona had the largest total area of any state but the smallest population. But with new military bases sprouting up left and right during World War II to train soldiers and pilots, people started flooding into Arizona and the population hasn't stopped growing since. Nowadays Arizona's a haven for retirees – about 10% of the total population are transplants soaking up the sunshine during their golden years. The warm winter climate and endless sunshine attract those looking to enjoy resort-style living year-round. But the state's also facing a "brain drain" as many young, college-educated professionals seek job opportunities and more affordable housing in others states, leaving Arizona with an older average population.

Arizona is nicknamed "The Grand Canyon State," and for good reason – that 277-mile-long, 18-mile-wide and mile-deep colorful canyon carved by the Colorado River is one of the most awe-inspiring natural wonders anywhere on the planet. It contains an incredible array of geological layers and rock formations from over 2 billion years of history on grand display. Humans have lived along Arizona's rivers for over 12,000 years. The Hohokam tribe built an ingenious irrigation system using gradient and gravity to move river water through a network of hundreds of miles of hand-dug canals for crop irrigation. They inhabited the area from about 200-1400 CE before mysteriously vanishing for unknown reasons, leaving behind a legacy of skilled masonry.

When Spanish conquistadors and missionaries arrived in the 1500s on expeditions to find the legendary "Seven Cities of Gold," they were followed by settlers from Mexico in the 1800s after the Mexican-American War. These pioneers expanded the existing Hohokam canals to grow all types of crops like alfalfa, fruit trees and cotton to sell. Homesteads soon turned into profitable farms and ranches with cattle ranching operations spreading across the state. Cattle drives became an iconic part of Arizona history, shaped by legendary figures like Wyatt Earp.

Man alive, Arizona's climate varies wildly across the different topographic regions! Summer in the low-lying deserts is a scorcher, with monsoon thunderstorms rolling up from the Gulf of Mexico bringing intense but spotty rainfall that can lead to dangerous flash floods rushing through arroyos and washes. Winters are mild in the southern half of the state while the northern mountainous areas get frequent snowstorms that occasionally shut schools down for snow days. Come spring, colorful wildflowers like Mexican gold poppies, spider lilies and Arizona bluebells bloom while folks keep an eye out for strong storms. Autumn is pleasant in the 70s and 80s but unpredictable, with heavy Pacific storms blowing through bringing howling winds and downpours.

Nearly every small town and city in Arizona has its own unique culture, evident in the traditional foods, annual festivals and architectural styles.

Native American tribes like the Navajo, Hopi, Apache and Tohono O'odham were the original inhabitants for thousands of years before Europeans arrived. They have many traditions and beliefs tied to the land and nature that endure today. The Spanish built Catholic missions and presidios and led migrations from Mexico up El Camino Real. You can see cultural influences blended into something uniquely Arizonan. Famous Arizona statesmen like Barry Goldwater embody that independent, rugged spirit.

Agriculture and tourism are pillars of the state's economy today. The river valleys dotted with citrus groves and vegetable farms produce everything from cotton to produce to feed the U.S. Incredible natural landscapes like the Grand Canyon, Monument Valley, Meteor Crater, and the red rocks of Sedona draw millions of tourists each year who pump money into the local economies. The numerous military bases around the state are economic engines too, contributing billions in revenue and tens of thousands of jobs. Major industries have developed around mining, aerospace engineering, microchip manufacturing, finance, and more.

So come visit this culturally vibrant southwestern state and experience the diverse landscapes and endless sunshine for yourself! From the epic Grand Canyon to the saguaro cactus forests to the majestic mountains, adventure awaits around every corner here in the Wild West. Whether you're looking for a relaxing desert retreat, an action-packed outdoor getaway or a journey into Native American history, Arizona has something for everyone. The state's motley assortment of adventurers, dreamers, and outlaws makes for an eclectic, welcoming vibe. With warm hospitality and breathtaking sights, an unforgettable journey awaits in Arizona!

The Map of Arizona

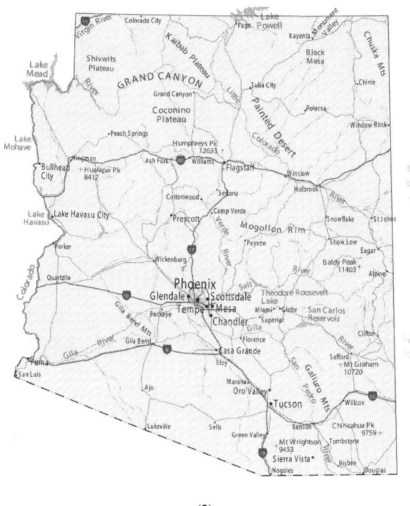

(2)

Why Visit Arizona?

It's a land of postcard-worthy views, majestic canyons, stunning desert landscapes, and charming mountain towns tucked away in pine forests. This state has a rich history stretching back to when Spanish conquistadors first set foot on the continent to the many Native peoples and ethnic groups that call Arizona home today.

Arizona's played host to some of America's most iconic battles and events over the years, like the skirmish at Picacho Pass and the shootout at the O.K. Corral in rowdy Tombstone. This rugged western state even starred in classic films like How the West Was Won.

There's so much natural beauty and adventure here, you have to see it yourself to really appreciate it, I tell you what. From the breathtakingly vast Grand Canyon to the red rock vistas of Sedona, Arizona's filled with postcard-worthy sights. And don't even get me started on all the critters! Javelina, roadrunners, coyotes - you never know what you'll spot roaming the desert.

Of course, it's the people that really make a place, and Arizona's no different. Folks from all walks of life - Native Americans, cowboys, artists, you name it - have blended together into a vibrant, welcoming culture all their own. Whether you want to dive into Hopi traditions or get your two-step on at a cowboy dancehall, Arizona's got you covered. With that fun-lovin' southwestern spirit, you can't help but feel a lifted mood here. From bustling Phoenix to quaint mountain towns like Bisbee, Arizona's cities, towns, and communities each have their own local flair. No matter who you are, you'll find your niche here.

When you're ready for a vacation offering adventure with a side of natural splendor, Arizona can't be beat. Go ahead, take a Jeep tour through the red rocks or spend the day discovering ancient petroglyphs along a canyon hike. Maybe take in a ball game or hit the slopes - the opportunities here are endless. However you choose to experience Arizona, a grand ol' time awaits. Yessiree, this state is plum full of beauty, excitement, and wide open spaces calling your name.

How To Use The Book

No matter your walk of life, you can find your own little slice of heaven in this gorgeous state. The rich, the poor, young, old, every race, gender and orientation - all are welcome to come to revel in Arizona's wonders. With an open mind and a bit o' research, incredible adventures await.

Seeing these landscapes yourself and soaking in their beauty is a heck of a lot more rewarding than scrolling through photos online or watching videos from afar. The hardest part is choosing where to start, 'cause there's just so dang much to experience! From the iconic Grand Canyon to Camelback Mountain overlooking Phoenix, Arizona is studded with stunning sites waiting to be discovered.

This guide covers 110 hand-picked adventures across the state perfect for nature lovers, history buffs, foodies and sightseers alike. Bring the whole family or just yourself - no matter your crew, you'll find exciting new activities. Spend a weekend or a whole month adventuring - with so much on offer, you'll never run out of fresh experiences. Use this book to plan your trip, then get to making those lifelong memories. I guarantee you'll be itching to return for more before you even leave!

Each entry gives you the lowdown on location, the ideal time to visit, GPS coordinates and interesting facts about the place. Flip to the suggested itineraries in the back for easy-to-follow routes to help make the most of your travels. Consider 'em a launchpad, then let your interests and whims carry you to the next scenic spot.

Whether you've got a few days or a few weeks to explore, this guide's got you covered with info to customize your journey. It'll spark conversation for that upcoming girls' getaway or family vacay too.

Truly, Arizona is blessed with some of God's greatest works. Do yourself a favor and witness 'em yourself. The landscapes will take your breath away. Go on now, pick your first adventure, map it out, then hit the road! Those bucket list memories won't make themselves. By the time your Arizona trip's done, you'll already be plotting your return.

AJO

Cabeza Prieta National Wildlife Refuge

(3)

Why You Should Visit:

Visit Cabeza Prieta National Wildlife Refuge to spot the bounding endangered Sonoran pronghorn antelope, admire ancient geoglyphs mysteriously etched into the barren desert pavement, and revel in the peaceful solitude of the rugged untamed Sonoran Desert landscape. With minimal amenities, this remote refuge offers an immersive wilderness experience.

Location:

1611 N 2nd Ave, Ajo, AZ 85321, USA

Best Time to Visit:

November through January's cooler, drier season

Pass/Permit:

No permit or fees required

Directions:

From Ajo, head west on N Taladro St, left on N 2nd Ave

GPS Coordinates: 32.3865° N, 112.8728° W

Nearest Town: Ajo, about 1.6 miles away

Interesting Facts: See rare desert bighorn sheep, a unique Arizona subspecies! Plus desert tortoises and endemic plants like yellow mouse ear flowers.

Organ Pipe Cactus National Monument

Why You Should Visit:

Marvel at the unique organ pipe cactus thriving in the wild, observe over 300 species of vibrant desert birds, and bask in the remote tranquility of this true Sonoran Desert escape. With rugged camping and endless solitude, this landscape offers natural rejuvenation.

Location:

10 Organ Pipe Dr, Ajo, AZ 85321, USA

Best Time to Visit:

November's cooler weather

Pass/Fees: $15 admission per vehicle valid for 7 days

Directions: From Ajo, head east on AZ-85 S/N Taladro St

GPS Coordinates: 32.0280° N, 112.8320° W

Nearest Town: Ajo, about 33 miles away

Interesting Facts: Rare organ pipe cacti grow here. Home to over 300 bird species.

APACHE JUNCTION

Goldfield Ghost Town

Why You Should Visit:

Step back in time at Goldfield Ghost Town, where you can explore Old West history and culture. This former mining town thrived during an 1890s gold rush before being abandoned in 1942. Now a preserved ghost town, Goldfield lets visitors see restored buildings, mine shafts, and more. Its rich heritage makes this a top destination.

Location:

4650 N Mammoth Mine Rd, Apache Junction, AZ 85119, USA

Best Time to Visit:

October onwards when the weather is cooler

Fees:

$10 adults, $9 seniors, $7 kids 5-12, under 5 free

Directions:

From Apache Junction, head northeast on N Apache Trail onto N Mammoth Mine Rd

GPS Coordinates:

33.4572°N, 111.4919°W

Nearest Town:

Apache Junction, about 8-10 minutes away

Interesting Facts: Goldfield contains replicated concrete foundations modeled after the original town, plus sewer covers and carved mine shafts.

Lost Dutchman State Park

Why You Should Visit:

Admire panoramic mountain views and explore desert trails at Lost Dutchman State Park. Situated on 138 acres in the Sonoran Desert, this state park offers fishing, picnicking, and mining history. Legend says a rich gold mine was discovered here by German immigrant Jacob Waltz, aka "The Lost Dutchman."

Location:

6109 N Apache Trail, Apache Junction, AZ 85119, USA

Best Time to Visit:

March to October for nice weather

Fees:

$10 per vehicle, $3 per person/bike

Directions:

From Apache Junction, head northeast on N Apache Trail onto AZ-88 E

GPS Coordinates:

33.4630°N, 111.4806°W

Nearest Town:

Apache Junction, about 8-15 minutes away

Interesting Facts:

This state park is named after the fabled Lost Dutchman gold mine, discovered by German immigrant Jacob Waltz in 1871.

BENSON

Kartchner Cavern State Park

Why You Should Visit:

Marvel at the country's largest natural limestone cavern, stretching 2.4 miles underground, at Kartchner Caverns State Park. This park also features a habitat with 65 subterranean creatures and the world's tallest active underground waterfall. Surrounded by Arizona's scenic desert landscapes, it's a must-see destination.

Location:

2980 AZ-90, Benson, AZ 85602, USA

Best Time to Visit:

Late September to early December to see fall colors

Fees:

$7 per vehicle, waived for tour ticket holders. Tours are $23, $13 ages 7-13, under 6 $5.

Directions:

From Benson, take I-10 W to AZ-90 S. After 9 miles, turn right to the park entrance.

GPS Coordinates:

31.2178°N, 110.0453°W

Nearest Town:

Benson, 15-20 minutes away

Interesting Facts:

This extensive show cave contains beautiful limestone formations like stalactites, stalagmites, columns, draperies and soda straws.

Quarles Art

Why You Should Visit:

View diverse artwork from renowned artists at Quarles Art Center, located in the Tohono O'odham Reservation. See how different cultures have influenced each other through modern paintings, sculptures, and more. Don't miss annual events like the Festival of the Arts.

Location:

Next to Wild Dogs, 1020 W 4th St, Benson, AZ 85602, USA

Best Time to Visit:

October or November for annual art events

Fees: $2 parking fee

Directions:

From Benson, head east on W Ash St, right on B Ave, right on W 4th St

GPS Coordinates:

33°29'35.8368"N, 111°55'40.4328"W

Nearest Towns:

Benson, 15-20 minutes away; Tohono O'odham Nation 30-35 minutes away

Interesting Facts: The center displays artwork by Andy Warhol, Roy Lichtenstein, Salvador Dalí and other renowned artists.

BISBEE

Center Town Old Bisbee, Arizona

Why You Should Visit:

Old Bisbee's Center Town transports you back to the 19th-century Wild West, with over 100 preserved buildings leftover from its mining boom days. Wander past remnants of old saloons, shops, and miner's cottages as ghosts of gunslingers roam the winding streets.

Location: 2 Tombstone Canyon, Bisbee, AZ 85603, USA

Best Time to Visit: Spring or summer for nice weather

Fees: $2 parking; $10 entry fee for non-residents

Directions: Head south on Tombstone Canyon toward Cantner Rd for 1.1 miles

GPS Coordinates: 31.4416°N, 109.9154°W

Nearest Town: Bisbee, 3-5 minutes away

Interesting Facts: Named a National Historic Landmark in 1977 for its well-preserved buildings.

Lavender Pit

Why You Should Visit:

The Lavender Pit offers an intriguing glimpse into Arizona's mining history. Tour this massive former copper mine, now a national landmark, and opt for a periodic ghost tour for extra intrigue. The views into the half-mile wide, 1,000 foot deep crater are striking. It's an impressive site for history buffs and anyone who enjoys marveling at large-scale industrial places.

Location: Bisbee, AZ 85603, USA

Best Time to Visit: Spring or summer for nice weather

Fees: $3 parking

Directions: From Bisbee, head north on Tombstone Canyon, left on AZ-80 E

GPS Coordinates: 31.4358°N, 109.9003°W

Nearest Town: Bisbee, 5-10 minutes away

Interesting Facts: This was the largest copper mine in Arizona when opened in 1883.

Muheim Heritage House

Why You Should Visit:

Experience Tohono O'odham Indian culture and traditions at Muheim Heritage House. See period rooms and cultural exhibits, and shop for local American Indian handicrafts. Don't miss special events like the annual pow wow.

Location: 207 Youngblood Hill Ave, Bisbee, AZ 85603, USA

Best Time to Visit: May pow wow or October festival

Fees: Donations accepted

Directions: From Bisbee, head south on Tombstone Canyon, right on Tombstone Canyon Rd, left on Howell Ave

GPS Coordinates: 31.4467°N, 109.9125°W

Nearest Town: Bisbee, 5-10 minutes away

Interesting Facts: Built-in 1996 by O'odham Artisans to showcase their culture.

Mule Pass Tunnel

Why You Should Visit:

Take a walk through Arizona's pioneering past by exploring the 3,160-foot Mule Pass Tunnel. Constructed in 1929 to provide safer passage to the mines, this may be the state's longest tunnel. Let your imagination wander as you trace the footsteps of determined miners who helped shape the region. Experience a piece of the frontier spirit that made history here.

Location: 1400-1524 AZ-80, Bisbee, AZ 85603, USA

Best Time to Visit: Spring or summer for nice weather

Fees: No fee

Directions: From Bisbee, head north on Tombstone Canyon, right on AZ-80 W

GPS Coordinates: 31.4564°N, 109.9409°W

Nearest Town: Bisbee, about 2 minutes away

Interesting Facts: The tunnel has been a filming location, like in the 1963 movie The 4 Horsemen of the Apocalypse.

BOUSE

East Cactus Plain Wilderness

Why You Should Visit:

Outdoor enthusiasts of all stripes should visit the scenic East Cactus Plain Wilderness to summit towering peaks, hike through serpentine canyons, and traverse stretches of the famed Route 66 Mother Road. Lace-up your hiking boots to wander desert trails past spiky cacti and creosote bushes. Hoist a leg over your mountain bike to cruise backcountry paths kept company by roaming coyotes, bobcats, and javelina.

Location: East Cactus Plain Wilderness, Bouse, AZ 85325, USA

Best Time to Visit: April through October for milder weather

Pass/Permit/Fees: No entrance fee; $5-$8 camping per person per night

Directions: From Douglas, head southeast on Broadway Ave, left on Main St, left on Rayder Ave, right on Swansea Rd

GPS Coordinates: 34.0667°N, 113.9438°W

Nearest Town: Bouse, about 20-25 minutes away

Interesting Facts: Diverse wildlife like javelina, coyotes, deer, bobcats, bears and many cacti types.

CAMP VERDE

Fort Verde State Historic Park

(4)

Why You Should Visit:

Step back in time at Fort Lowell Museum, home to preserved 19th-century buildings and artifacts that immerse you in frontier military life. Wander past adobe ruins, imagining clashes between soldiers and Native tribes. For the full experience, visit the Living History Museum where reenactors vividly bring the Arizona frontier story to life.

Location: 125 E Hollamon St, Camp Verde, AZ 86322, USA

Best Time to Visit: June through September when everything's open

Fees: $7 adults, $4 youth ages 7-13, free under 6

Directions: From Camp Verde, north on Main St, right on E Hollamon St

GPS Coordinates: 34.5641°N, 111.8521°W

Nearest Town: Camp Verde, 1-5 minutes away

Interesting Facts: The fort was named for George T. Verde and used until 1874.

Montezuma Castle National Monument

Why You Should Visit:

Marvel at the ancient Sinagua cliff dwelling, Montezuma Castle, perched dramatically on a limestone cliff. Explore this well-preserved stone and mud structure dating back to 1100 AD. As one of the oldest cliff dwellings in North America, it offers a window into the past.

Location: Montezuma Castle Rd, Camp Verde, AZ

Best Time to Visit: April through October for nice weather

Fees: $10 adults, $5 ages 7-15, free under 6

Directions: From Camp Verde, north on Main St, right on Montezuma Castle Rd

GPS Coordinates: 34.6116°N, 111.8350°W

Nearest Town: Camp Verde, 7-10 minutes away

Interesting Facts: Walls insulated with mud and whitewashed with lime plaster.

CHINLE

Canyon De Chelly National Monument

Why You Should Visit:

Get ready for your jaw to drop at Canyon de Chelly's breathtaking views. This Navajo sacred site is home to the towering 800-foot Spider Rock spire and sheer sandstone cliffs covered in ancient rock art. As you explore the canyon's rich history and geologic formations, you'll quickly understand why it's considered such a special monument.

Location: Canyon de Chelly National Monument, Chinle, AZ 86503, USA

Best Time to Visit: Summer to hike, join ranger talks and wildlife tours

Fees: $1 per person for Spider Rock and Trail of Time hikes

Directions: From Chinle, north on Main St, left on Indian Rte 7, stay on Indian Rte 64

GPS Coordinates: 36.1191°N, 109.3197°W

Nearest Town: Chinle, about 5 minutes away

Interesting Facts: Home to Navajo people for thousands of years. Over 450 sites were occupied in the 14th century.

Hope Arch

Why You Should Visit:

Behold Hope Arch, an astonishing natural sandstone marvel that steals the scene. This graceful arch may just be the Southwest's most photogenic, framing inspiring vistas that serve as the perfect backdrop for photos and weddings. As you admire its striking beauty, you'll understand why so many consider it the most beautiful arch around. Hope Arch highlights nature's artistry at its finest.

Location: Hope Arch, Chinle, AZ 86503, USA

Best Time to Visit: Mornings in April-October

Fees: No fee, just need a driver's license to drive near the arch

Directions: From Chinle, north on Main St, right on Indian Rte 7, left on US-191 N, left on C669

GPS: 36.2021397°N, 109.6890771°W

Nearest Town: Chinle, about 20-25 minutes away

Interesting Facts: Formed from natural sandstone erosion over time.

CIBECUE

Cibecue Creek

Why You Should Visit:

Escape to Cibecue Creek, a pristine desert oasis nestled in a dramatic canyon setting. Revel in the clear waters and granite-lined banks perfect for swimming, wading or a waterside picnic. Hike among fragrant sagebrush and along the creek to breathtaking overlooks. With its gorgeous scenery and inviting waters, Cibecue Creek offers the ultimate spot to recharge in nature's beauty.

Location: Cibecue Creek, Chinle, AZ 86503, USA

Best Time to Visit: April through September for warm, dry weather

Fees: $30 permit per day for hiking

Directions: From Chinle, head west on W Cibecue Rd, right on N Tessay

GPS Coordinates: 34.2966°N, 109.2106°W

Nearest Town: Tombstone, about 10-12 minutes away

Interesting Facts: Formed in the 1990s by damming irrigation canals that were built during the Depression. The area was previously used for growing alfalfa.

CLARKDALE

Arizona Copper Art Museum

Why You Should Visit:

Discover over 4,000 Native American artifacts, historic mining relics, and dazzling mineral sculptures at the Arizona Copper Art Museum in Clarkdale. One of the state's most stunning museums, it showcases regional history through copper, silver, and gold artworks. Wander through the collection for an insider's look into Arizona's cultural and industrial heritage.

Location: 849 Main St, Clarkdale, AZ 86324, USA

Best Time to Visit: Spring to enjoy blooms and seasonal events

Fees: $9.75 adults, discounted rates for seniors, students, and kids

Directions: From Clarkdale, north on Main St, right on S 9th St, left on S 6th St

GPS Coordinates: 34.7711°N, 112.0568°W

Nearest Town: Clarkdale, about 5 minutes away

Interesting Facts: Founded in 1976 by Bob Holbrook to showcase Arizona artworks.

Verde River Access

Why You Should Visit:

Swim, wade, or picnic at Verde River Access. This peaceful spot in Clarkdale has a small swimming hole, old cliffs, rock formations and streaks of white water set against lush green foliage.

Location: Verde River Access, Clarkdale, AZ 86324, USA

Best Time to Visit: Late spring or summer for swimming

Fees: $5 parking fee

Directions: From Clarkdale, east on Main St, right on S 9th St, left on S 6th St

GPS: 34.7663°N, 112.0373°W

Nearest Town: Tombstone, 4-10 minutes away

Interesting Facts: Named Verde for its green riverside foliage. First discovered by a surveyor in 1883.

FLAGSTAFF

Buffalo Park

(5)

Why You Should Visit:

Explore Old West architecture and ride horses at sprawling Buffalo Park outside Flagstaff. Take a scenic wagon ride or enjoy panoramic views of the San Francisco Peaks. With activities for all, it's a can't-miss destination.

Location: 2400 N Gemini Rd, Flagstaff, AZ 86004, USA

Best Time to Visit: May through October for pleasant weather

Fees: $10 adults, $5 youth, free under 6

Directions: From Flagstaff, east on S Humphreys St, left on N Gemini Rd

GPS Coordinates: 35.2185°N, 111.6330°W

Nearest Town: Flagstaff, 6-10 minutes away

Interesting Facts: Named for the visible San Francisco Peaks according to Native American tradition.

Cococino Lava River Cave

Why You Should Visit:

Delve into the mesmerizing underground realm of Cococino Lava River Cave, forged eons ago by volcanic activity. Nicknamed the "Grand Canyon of the East," this extensive natural cave dazzles with otherworldly lava formations. As you venture deep below the earth's surface, be awestruck by dramatic geological features and glimpses into the power of nature. Cococino Lava River Cave offers an adventure into Arizona's awe-inspiring past.

Location: 171B Forest Rd, Flagstaff, AZ 86001, USA

Best Time to Visit: Late March to early November for comfortable cave temperatures

Fees: No fee, age limits apply

Directions: From Flagstaff, west on Historic Route 66, right on N Humphreys St, left on N Fort Valley Rd

GPS: 35.3424°N, 111.8363°W

Nearest Town: Flagstaff, 40-50 minutes away

Interesting Facts: First recorded in 1881 but believed carved by lava 10,000+ years ago.

Downtown Flagstaff

Why You Should Visit:

Flagstaff's vibrant downtown overflows with culture and character. Stroll past unique shops, locally-owned restaurants, and charming galleries that showcase the city's artistic spirit. Visit in fall when dazzling foliage creates a picturesque backdrop for cultural events hosted by the spirited community. From the eclectic local business scene to the welcoming small-town feel, Flagstaff's lively downtown offers an authentic taste of Northern Arizona.

Location: 6 E Aspen Ave Suite 200, Flagstaff, AZ 86001, USA

Best Time to Visit: Fall to see incredible leaf colors

Fees: Free, $5 parking

Directions: From Flagstaff, east on S San Francisco St, left on N Birch Ave, left on E Aspen Ave

GPS: 35.1987°N, 111.6483°W

Nearest Town: Flagstaff, 5 minutes away

Interesting Facts: One of Arizona's most diverse cities with deep Native American, Mexican, and Chinese heritage.

Frances Short Pond

Why You Should Visit:

Escape to the tranquility of Frances Short Pond, a spring-fed oasis just outside Flagstaff perfect for anglers and nature lovers alike. Cast for trout in the pond's pristine waters or spot birds among the ponderosa pines surrounding this serene fishing hole. With its exceptional trout habitat and idyllic natural setting, Frances Short Pond promises rejuvenating outdoor recreation in a gorgeous mountain backdrop.

Location: Frances Short Pond, Flagstaff, AZ 86001, USA

Best Time to Visit: March to August fishing season

Fees: $4 fishing fee for adults 17+, licenses required

Directions: From Flagstaff, east on S San Francisco St, left on E

Saddlebag Dr, left on N Saddlebag Dr

GPS: 35.1852°N, 111.6256°W

Nearest Town: Flagstaff, 7-10 minutes away

Interesting Facts: Named after a revered Native American grandmother who fished here.

Fort Tuthill County Park

Why You Should Visit:

Nestled amidst ponderosa pines, Fort Tuthill County Park entices outdoor enthusiasts with abundant recreation. Pitch a tent at the campground, hike miles of scenic trails, and cool off with a swim during a warm summer day. With its mix of natural beauty and amenities, this vast park provides the ideal Northern Arizona getaway for nature lovers and families alike. **Location**: 2446 Ft Tuthill Lp, Flagstaff, AZ 86005, USA

Best Time to Visit: May through October for nice weather

Fees: $6 vehicles, $4.25 hikers, $2.50 bikers

Directions: From Flagstaff, west on Historic Route 66, left on N Fort Valley Rd, right on Fort Tuthill Loop Rd

GPS: 35.1415°N, 111.6913°W

Nearest Town: Flagstaff, 15-20 minutes away

Interesting Facts: Named for Arizona's State Forester Charles Tuthill

who served from 1919-1942.

Lowell Observatory

Why You Should Visit:

Step into astronomy history at Flagstaff's Lowell Observatory, where Pluto and other planets were first spotted. Tour the iconic facility and look through the same telescope lenses used by pioneering astronomers. Guided tours and exhibits showcase the observatory's legacy of cosmic discovery and stellar views that have inspired generations of star gazers. **Location**: 1400 W Mars Hill Rd, Flagstaff, AZ 86001, USA

Best Time to Visit: Year-round, but summer nights are ideal

Fees: $29 adults, discounted rates for students, seniors, and kids

Directions: From Flagstaff, east on I-40, exit 137A onto Flagstaff Rd

GPS: 35.2029°N, 111.6646°W

Nearest Town: Camp Verde, about 38 miles away

Interesting Facts: Named for astronomer Percival Lowell, first to observe Uranus in 1892 with his own telescope.

Riordan Mansion State Historic Park

Why You Should Visit:

Nestled among ponderosa pines, this gorgeous mansion belonged to successful mining magnates Timothy and Michael Riordan. Tour the historic residence and experience what prosperous family life was like in early 20th-century Flagstaff. With its exceptional craftsmanship and tranquil setting, Riordan Mansion offers an intimate look into Flagstaff's pioneer heritage.

Location: 409 W Riordan Rd, Flagstaff, AZ 86001, USA

Best Time to Visit: October and April for special events

Fees: $12 adults, $6 youth, free under 6

Directions: From Flagstaff, east on Historic Route 66

GPS Coordinates: 35.1874°N, 111.6595°W

Nearest Town: Flagstaff, 5 minutes away

Interesting Facts: Stone and timber were locally sourced from the owners' 2,400 acre estate.

Sunset Crater Volcano National Monument

Why You Should Visit:

Marvel at the immense volcanic crater formed by a 1045 AD eruption at Sunset Crater Volcano. One of just three hikeable volcanic sites in the U.S., it offers rare up-close views. Hike the popular trails circling the 2.4-mile-wide crater.

Location: 6082 Sunset Crater Road, Flagstaff, AZ 86004

Best Time to Visit: Early August for spectacular sunsets

Fees: $25 per vehicle, $10 seniors, free under 16. Hiking permit extra.

Directions: From Flagstaff, south on US-89, right on Forest Road 602

GPS Coordinates: 35°22'09.0"N, 111°32'36.6"W

Nearest Town: Winslow, about 20 miles away

Interesting Facts: Site of a 1700 battle between Native Americans and the US Army.

Walnut Canyon National Monument

Why You Should Visit:

Make a stop at the cliff dwellings tucked into Walnut Canyon's dramatic limestone walls. Home to Sinagua people 700 years ago, this serene natural site near Flagstaff has hiking trails, wildlife, wildflowers and amazing stargazing.

Location: 3 Walnut Canyon Rd, Flagstaff, AZ 86004

Best Time to Visit: November for the star-gazing picnic

Fees: $25 per vehicle

Directions: From Flagstaff, east on Historic Route 66, right on Ponderosa Pkwy, left on I-40 E, exit 204

GPS Coordinates: 35.1690°N, 111.5043°W

Nearest Town: Flagstaff, 15-20 minutes away

Interesting Facts: Evidence of 100+ rooms built by the Sinagua people 700 years ago.

Wupatki National Monument

(6)

Why You Should Visit:

Explore over 500 ancient petroglyphs and native dwellings at Wupatki National Monument near Flagstaff. Formed by volcanic eruptions, this site offers a glimpse into Sinagua and Ancestral Puebloan culture through rock art, ruins and artifacts.

Location: 25137 North Wupatki Lane, Flagstaff, AZ 86004

Best Time to Visit: March to November for nice weather

Fees: $25 per vehicle

Directions: From Flagstaff, east on Historic Route 66, right on N 89, right on Loop Rd

GPS Coordinates: 35.5600°N, 111.3935°W

Nearest Town: Flagstaff, 35-40 minutes away

Interesting Facts: Wupatki means "house of the rock" in Hopi language. Evidence of native habitation from 500-1250 AD.

GANADO

Ganado Lake

Why You Should Visit:

Ganado Lake is a little slice of heaven right here in Arizona's high desert. This tranquil blue gem is tucked amongst the dynamically hued mesas, canyons, and ridges of Navajo country. Make your way up to these parts and soak in the peaceful easy vibes of this desert oasis. Glide across glistening waters on a kayak, cast your line for a big ol' trout, or spread out a picnic blanket along the sandy banks. Bring the whole family to splash around in the lake or kick back and unwind as the tension melts away.

Location: Ganado Lake, Ganado, AZ 86505

Best Time to Visit: April to October for sunny weather

Fees: No entrance fee

Directions: From Ganado, south on Post Office Rd, left on AZ-264 E

GPS Coordinates: 35.7368°N, 109.5181°W

Nearest Town: Ganado, 6-10 minutes away

Interesting Facts: Created in the 1930s by damming a natural reservoir. Revitalized for recreation in the 1990s.

GILBERT

Freestone District Park

Why You Should Visit:

This fantastic park features a mini amusement park, skate park, fishing pond, playground, pool, and more to enjoy year-round. With activities for all interests and ages, it's a great place to let kids burn off energy or create special memories together. Freestone District Park truly has something for everyone seeking outdoor adventure and fun.

Location: 1045 E Juniper Ave, Gilbert, AZ 85234, USA

Best Time to Visit: April to October for sunny weather

Fees: Pool and fishing passes - $4 adults, $2 kids

Directions: From Gilbert, north on N Ash St, left on W Page Ave, left on N Gilbert Rd, left on E Elliot Rd

GPS: 33.3593°N, 111.7671°W

Nearest Town: Gilbert, 6-10 minutes away

Interesting Facts: Opened in 1993 as part of a Gilbert community expansion project. Over 1 million annual visitors.

Riparian Preserve At Water Ranch

Why You Should Visit:

Explore 1,000+ acres with trails and educational signs along the Verde River at Riparian Preserve at Water Ranch. See wildlife, native plants, canyons, and fossils at this natural oasis near Gilbert.

Location: 2757 E Guadalupe Rd, Gilbert, AZ 85234, USA

Best Time to Visit: Open year-round

Fees: No entrance fee

Directions: From Gilbert, north on N Ash St, right on W Page Ave, left on N Gilbert Rd, right on E Guadalupe Rd

GPS Coordinates: 33.3644°N, 111.7347°W

Nearest Town: Gilbert, 13-15 minutes away

Interesting Facts: Dedicated in 1995 honoring former Gilbert Mayor Peter Gilbert and wife Laura.

Water Tower Plaza

Why You Should Visit:

Relax at Grass-filled Water Tower Plaza in Gilbert. Enjoy the small lake, mountain views, and water features at this peaceful park. The perfect spot for a sunny day outside.

Location: 45 W Page Ave, Gilbert, AZ 85233, USA

Best Time to Visit: April to October for water recreation

Fees: No entrance fee

Directions: From Gilbert, north on N Ash St, left on W Page Ave, left on N Gilbert Rd

GPS Coordinates: 33.3546°N, 111.7907°W

Nearest Town: Gilbert, 1-5 minutes away

Interesting Facts: Dedicated in 1998 honoring former Gilbert Mayor Peter Gilbert and wife Laura.

GLOBE

Besh-Ba-Gowah Museum

Why You Should Visit:

Learn about Native American history and culture at the Besh-Ba-Gowah Museum in Globe. Founded in 1984 with donated artifacts and documents, it offers a 120-year look into the past. Thousands of photographs, objects and pieces showcase the area's rich heritage. Check out wagons and horses around the town square on Sundays too. Named for the original Native term meaning "place of good water," this is a top spot to immerse yourself in the region's roots.

Location: 1324 S Jesse Hayes Rd, Globe, AZ 85501

Best Time to Visit: Sundays for wagon rides on the town square

Fees: $5 adults, $4 seniors 65+, free under 12

Directions: From Globe, northeast on W Cottonwood St, right on S Broad St, right on Ruiz Canyon Rd, left on S Jesse Hayes Rd

GPS Coordinates: 35.73341°N, 113.81383°W

Nearest Town: Globe, 4-8 minutes away

Interesting Facts: Founded in 1984 by the AZ Historical Society of Globe-Miami Inc. Became part of the Historical Society of Pinal County in 1996.

HOLBROOK

Rainbow Forest Museum

Why You Should Visit:

Learn about the area's natural history at Holbrook's Rainbow Forest Museum. See displays of pottery, glass, jewelry and other artifacts used by past inhabitants. Enjoy a scavenger hunt and other fun, educational activities too.

Location: 6618 Petrified Forest Rd, Holbrook, AZ 86025

Best Time to Visit: October to April to see animal exhibits

Fees: No entrance fee

Directions: From Holbrook, west on Navajo Blvd, left on Apache Ave, left on US-180 E, left on Petrified Forest Rd

GPS Coordinates: 34°48'54.5508"N, 109°51'56.9628"W

Nearest Town: Holbrook, about 20 miles away

Interesting Facts: Founded in 1997 by the AZ Historical Society of Pinal County. Named for the colorful wooded area and nearby petrified forest.

JEROME

Audrey Headframe Park

Why You Should Visit:

Explore mining history and nature at Audrey Headframe Park. See mineral and fossil displays, hike trails along Sawmill Creek, and take in panoramic views from the headframe. A great way to experience Jerome's past.

Location: 55 Douglas Rd, Jerome, AZ 86331

Best Time to Visit: April to October for nice weather

Fees: No entrance fee, donations appreciated

Directions: From Jerome, east on Main St, left on Douglas Rd

GPS Coordinates: 34.7537°N, 112.1126°W

Nearest Town: Jerome, 1.3 miles away

Interesting Facts: Named after Audrey McCulloch, wife of a former park superintendent.

Jerome State Historic Park

Why You Should Visit:

Step back in time at Jerome State Historic Park. Founded in 1943, it preserves Jerome's buildings, history and culture through artifact displays. Learn about this former mining boom town on a stroll through the streets. **Location**: 100 Douglas Rd, Jerome, AZ 86331

Best Time to Visit: May to October for nice weather

Fees: $7 adults, $4 ages 7-13, free under 6

Directions: From Jerome, east on Main St, left on Douglas Rd, right on E Burns St

GPS Coordinates: 34.7536°N, 112.1112°W

Nearest Town: Jerome, 1.3 miles away

Interesting Facts: Explore Jerome's rise as a mining town and its attempts to rebuild after the 1917 flood.

KAYENTA

Navajo Shadehouse Museum

Why You Should Visit:

Discover Kayenta's heritage at Navajo Shadehouse Museum. Founded in 1974, it displays pottery, tools, clothing and other artifacts from ancient regional communities. See Navajo artworks and learn about Native American life at this top local history spot.

Location: US-160, Kayenta, AZ 86033

Best Time to Visit: May to March for dry weather, or October to April for cooler temps

Fees: Free admission

Directions: From Kayenta, east on Comb Ridge Rd, right on US-163 S, right on US-160 W

GPS Coordinates: 36.7077°N, 110.2531°W

Nearest Town: Kayenta, about 2 miles away

Interesting Facts: Opened in 1979 on a $25,000 budget raised entirely from community donations.

LAKE HAVASU CITY

London Bridge

Why You Should Visit:

See this iconic Lake Havasu City landmark, the London Bridge. Reminiscent of the original 19th century bridge, it features shops, restaurants and replicas of London buildings like the Tower Bridge. A must-see for tourists that captures English charm.

Location: 1340 McCulloch Blvd N, Lake Havasu City, AZ 86403

Best Time to Visit: Mornings or evenings in summer, or winter months to avoid crowds

Fees: No entrance fee, tours available

Directions: From Lake Havasu City, northwest on Mescal Loop, left on McCulloch Blvd N

GPS Coordinates: 34.4716°N, 114.3475°W

Nearest Town: Lake Havasu City, 1.8 miles away

Interesting Facts: The original London Bridge was built in 1831 before being relocated to Arizona in the 1960s.

NOGALES

Patagonia Lake State Park

(7)

Why You Should Visit:

Enjoy Arizona's natural beauty at Patagonia Lake State Park near Nogales. Picnic, camp, or swim at this scenic spot with lakes, streams, meadows, and abundant wildlife. A perfect place to relax outdoors and take in gorgeous scenery.

Location: 400 Patagonia Lake Rd, Nogales, AZ 85621

Best Time to Visit: Spring through fall

Fees: $15-20 per vehicle daily

Directions: From Nogales, northwest on N Wayside Dr, right on AZ-82 E, left on N Mexico Rd

GPS Coordinates: 31.4883°N, 110.8538°W

Nearest Town: Nogales, 22-30 miles away

Interesting Facts: Established in the 1880s by Joseph D. Poole before being donated to Arizona as a state park.

Nogales Border Plaza

Why You Should Visit:

Find dining, music, and shopping at Nogales' lively Border Plaza. Concerts and events are often held in this popular plaza packed with restaurants, souvenir shops, and boutiques. A great place for entertainment.

Location: 89-159 N Morley Ave, Nogales, AZ 85621

Best Time to Visit: May to October for smaller crowds

Fees: Possible parking fees

Directions: From Nogales, northwest on N Wayside Dr, right on N Morley Ave

GPS Coordinates: 31.3344°N, 110.9406°W

Nearest Town: Nogales, 2 minutes away

Interesting Facts: Originally built in the 1930s as a marketplace, now caters more to tourists.

PAGE

Antelope Canyon

Why You Should Visit:

Make a stop at the Antelope Canyon's stunning slot canyon scenery near Page. Formed by the Colorado River over time, it contains beautiful winding rock formations, trails and picture-perfect vistas. A scenic wonderland for hiking and exploring.

Location: Navajo Tribal Park, Page, AZ

Best Time to Visit: Summer if you don't mind crowds

Fees: Tours required plus $8 Navajo permit

Directions: From Page, southwest on AZ-89, south on AZ-260, west on Navajo Dr

GPS Coordinates: 36.8619°N, 111.3743°W

Nearest Town: Page, about 10 minutes away

Interesting Facts: Known as "The Eye of the Storm" for its steep, narrow red sandstone walls in places.

Carl Hayden Visitor Center

Why You Should Visit:

Revel in the scenic beauty and adventures of Carl Hayden Visitor Center near Page. Hike, fish, boat and more while admiring views of the Colorado River, Natural Bridge, Phantom Ranch and beyond. A playground for outdoor fun.

Location: US-89, Page, AZ 86040

Best Time to Visit: April-October for nice weather, November-March to avoid crowds

Fees: Free admission

Directions: From Page, northeast on Navajo Dr, left on Lake Powell Blvd, left on Coppermine Rd, right on AZ-98 W, left on US-89 S

GPS Coordinates: 36.9357°N, 111.4858°W

Nearest Town: Page, 5-10 minutes away

Interesting Facts: Named for Senator Carl Hayden, who helped establish the National Park Service.

Horseshoe Bend

Why You Should Visit:

Here you can admire the breathtaking cliff carved by the Colorado River over time at the famous Horseshoe Bend near Page. This natural wonder's stunning views draw photographers and sightseers galore.

Location: Horseshoe Bend Rd, Page, AZ 86040

Best Time to Visit: May to October for ideal weather

Fees: $10 per vehicle, $5 per motorcycle

Directions: From Page, northeast on Navajo Dr, right on Lake Powell Blvd, left on US-89 S, right on Page Pkwy, right on Horseshoe Bend Rd

GPS Coordinates: 36.966°N, 110.317°W

Nearest Town: Page, about 5 miles away

Interesting Facts: Popular Hollywood filming location mentioned in movies like Dances with Wolves.

Lake Powell

Why You Should Visit:

Soak up the endless adventures and scenery at Lake Powell near Page. Formed by Glen Canyon Dam, it has 1,000 miles of winding shoreline. Hike, boat, fish, camp and explore this desert oasis.

Location: Page, AZ 86040

Best Time to Visit: June to October for warm weather and high water

Fees: $30 for 7 days, covers one vehicle and passengers

Directions: From Page, northwest on US-89 N

GPS Coordinates: 36.9147°N, 111.4558°W

Nearest Town: Page, minutes away

Interesting Facts: One of the largest man-made lakes in the U.S., named for Colorado River explorer John Wesley Powell.

Water Holes Canyon

Why You Should Visit:

Journey through the narrow, dark passages of naturally carved Waterholes Canyon. Photographers flock to capture beams of light in the slot canyon near Page. Formed by thousands of years of erosion, it's a unique landscape.

Location: Waterholes Canyon, Page, AZ 86040

Best Time to Visit: March to November for moderate temperatures

Fees: Guided tours are around $65-$81 per person

Directions: From Page, northeast on Navajo Dr, right on Lake Powell Blvd, left on Coppermine Rd, right on AZ-98 W, left on US-89 S

GPS Coordinates: 36.8467°N, 111.5247°W

Nearest Town: Page, about 10 minutes away

Interesting Facts: Home to geyser-like water spouts. Near the larger Antelope Canyon.

PEACH SPRINGS

Grand Canyon Caverns

Why You Should Visit:

Explore the largest dry caverns in the U.S. at Grand Canyon Caverns near Peach Springs. Tour the underground world, dine at restaurants, or stay overnight in these vast limestone caves near Lake Powell and the Colorado River.

Location: AZ-66, Peach Springs, AZ 86434

Best Time to Visit: May to September for moderate temperatures and smaller crowds

Fees: $25.95 adults, discounted rates for seniors, youth, and kids

Directions: From Peach Springs, east on AZ-66, right on Grand Canyon Caverns Rd

GPS Coordinates: 35.5287°N, 113.2310°W

Nearest Town: Peach Springs, about 12 miles away

Interesting Facts: Features a natural underground river guests can experience.

Hualapai River Runners

Why You Should Visit:

Revel in water sports and adventures along the Hualapai River at Lake Powell. Rent kayaks, canoes, paddleboards, jet skis and more, or go fishing. Stay at the scenic lakeside lodge nearby. The perfect summertime play spot.

Location: 900 East, AZ-66, Peach Springs, AZ 86434

Best Time to Visit: April to October for ideal weather

Fees: Vary by activity, from $14/hour to $81/day

Directions: From Peach Springs, east on Historic Route 66, right on AZ-66, left on AZ-66

GPS Coordinates: 35.5287°N, 113.2310°W

Nearest Town: Peach Springs, about 1 minute away

Interesting Facts: Named for the Hualapai tribe native to Arizona and Nevada.

PHOENIX

Arizona Science Center

(8)

Why You Should Visit:

Discover science, tech and math at the Arizona Science Center's hands-on exhibits. Meet astronauts during Space Week, see ever-changing shows in the Planetarium, and take classes. A nonprofit spreading STEM fun for all ages.

Location: 600 E Washington St, Phoenix, AZ 85004

Best Time to Visit: June through August for outdoor activities

Fees: $21.95 adults, $15.95 ages 3-17, free under 2

Directions: From downtown Phoenix, take I-10 west, exit at Monroe St, left on 2nd Ave, left on Washington St

GPS Coordinates: 33.4485°N, 112.0662°W

Nearest Town: Tempe, about 17-19 minutes away

Interesting Facts: Planetarium shows every 15 minutes about space.

Camelback Mountain

Why You Should Visit:

Hike or drive up Camelback Mountain for phenomenal views over Phoenix. Its summit offers breathtaking panoramas from Lake Powell to Mexico. The perfect vantage point to watch the sunset over the city.

Location: 4925 E McDonald Dr, Phoenix, AZ 85253

Best Time to Visit: November-March for ideal hiking weather

Fees: Free entry

Directions: From Phoenix Airport, take Route 51 north to Camelback Rd in Glendale

GPS Coordinates: 33.5151°N, 111.9619°W

Nearest Town: Scottsdale, about 15-20 minutes away

Interesting Facts: Camelback Mountain Village has sunrise and sunset viewing decks.

Cave Buttes Recreation Area

Why You Should Visit:

Hike, bike, birdwatch and explore Cave Buttes Recreation Area's scenic trails and uniquely named lakes. This wildlife haven near Phoenix offers fishing spots and sweeping views atop its rocky flat-topped butte.

Location: N 7th St & E Happy Valley Rd, Phoenix, AZ 85024

Best Time to Visit: Summer for events and activities

Fees: $3 entrance, $85 annual pass, $8 camping

Directions: From Phoenix, west on Washington St, right on Black Canyon Hwy, right on AZ-101 Loop W

GPS Coordinates: 33.7103°N, 112.0497°W

Nearest Town: Phoenix, about 30 minutes away

Interesting Facts: Named for a past Native American tribe meaning "the rocks that chop enemies."

Civic Space Park

Why You Should Visit:

Enjoy open green space, modern sculptures and historical buildings at Civic Space Park in downtown Phoenix. Stroll through this revitalized area packed with interpretive panels about the past.

Location: 424 N Central Ave, Phoenix, AZ 85004

Best Time to Visit: December through February to avoid heat

Fees: Free, donations accepted

Directions: From Phoenix, west on Washington St, right on 3rd Ave, right on Van Buren St, left on Central Ave

GPS Coordinates: 33.4534°N, 112.0747°W

Nearest Town: Phoenix, about 5 minutes away

Interesting Facts: "Light" sculpture created by artist Beverly Pepper.

Desert Botanical Garden

Why You Should Visit:

Spot at 10,000+ plant species from around the world at Desert Botanical Garden. See acres of native cacti, poppies, agave and more. Don't miss the iconic musical pipers!

Location: 1201 N Galvin Pkwy, Phoenix, AZ 85008

Best Time to Visit: April-October for peak plant life

Fees: $24.95-$29.95 adults, $14.95-$16.95 ages 3-17, under 2 free

Directions: From Phoenix Airport, take I-10 west, exit at Scottsdale Rd, left on Galvin Pkwy

GPS Coordinates: 33.4615°N, 111.9441°W

Nearest Town: Scottsdale, about 10 minutes away

Interesting Facts: Home to a biotic pyramid with desert life like agave.

Encanto Park

Why You Should Visit:

Nature lovers should head to Encanto Park in Phoenix to enjoy lakes, trails, playgrounds and more without leaving the city. Check out the visitor center for info on this sprawling park's history and surroundings. With activities galore, it's a can't-miss urban oasis.

Location: 2605 N 15th Ave, Phoenix, AZ 85007

Best Time to Visit: April-October for events and festivals

Fees: Free admission

Directions: From Phoenix, west on Washington St, right on 7th Ave, left on Jackson St, left on 7th Ave, right on Encanto Blvd

GPS Coordinates: 33.4743°N, 112.0892°W

Nearest Town: Phoenix, less than 10 minutes away

Interesting Facts: At 2,400 acres, it holds the record for the world's largest city park. It was once part of a 35,000 acre ranch.

Heard Museum

Why You Should Visit:

Immerse yourself in Native American culture through art, workshops, lectures and events at Phoenix's acclaimed Heard Museum. Dedicated to advancing American Indian art and teachings, it's a top destination to learn.

Location: 2301 N Central Ave, Phoenix, AZ 85004

Best Time to Visit: June-August for free outdoor programs

Fees: $25 adults, discounts for seniors, students, tribes and kids

Directions: From Phoenix, west on I-10, exit Indian School Rd, right on Indian School Rd, left on Central Ave

GPS Coordinates: 33.4726°N, 112.0722°W

Nearest Town: Scottsdale, about 30 minutes away

Interesting Facts: Houses a replica of a 3000 year old Hohokam Indian dwelling.

Heritage And Science Park

Why You Should Visit:

Discover interactive science, tech and art exhibits at Heritage and Science Park in downtown Phoenix. See how the world works in unique ways. Don't miss the concerts, events and rocket-themed mini golf!

Location: 500 E Washington St, Phoenix AZ 85004

Best Time to Visit: October for autumn festivals

Fees: $19.95 adults, $14.95 ages 4-12, free under 3

Directions: From Phoenix, west on I-10, exit Monroe St, left on Monroe St, right on 2nd Ave, left on Washington St

GPS Coordinates: 33.4500°N, 112.0658°W

Nearest Town: Tempe, about 20 minutes away

Interesting Facts: Features two walk-through spaceships and an 18-hole mini golf course modeled after a rocket.

Hole In The Rock

(9)

Why You Should Visit:

See the unusual worn rock formation with three points and a large hole you can climb through at Hole in the Rock in Phoenix's Papago Park. A fun place for pictures and exploration.

Location: 625 N Galvin Pkwy, Phoenix, AZ 85008

Best Time to Visit: November-March for ideal weather, or April-October to avoid rain

Fees: Free admission

Directions: From Phoenix, west on I-10, exit Grand Ave, right on Grand Ave, left on Palm Ln, right on Galvin Pkwy

GPS Coordinates: 33.4565°N, 111.9453°W

Nearest Town: Tempe, about 15 minutes away

Interesting Facts: Small holes in the ground were used by Native Americans to grind food.

Phoenix Bat Cave

Why You Should Visit:

Explore the world's largest bat cave, home to 25+ species, on a tour at Phoenix's Dunlap Park. See these essential creatures up close in their natural habitat within the city.

Location: 3698-3694 E Colter St, Phoenix, AZ 85018

Best Time to Visit: April-October when bats are active

Fees: Free admission

Directions: From Phoenix, west on Washington St, left on 7th Ave, right on I-10 E, exit AZ-202, exit 40th St, left on 40th St

GPS Coordinates: 33.5145°N, 112.0013°W

Nearest Town: Phoenix, less than 20 minutes away

Interesting Facts: Some bats here weigh up to 1 lb and hunt insects at dusk.

Phoenix Zoo

Why You Should Visit:

See 1,400+ animals from around the world at the Phoenix Zoo, the largest privately owned nonprofit zoo in the U.S. Check out the extensive mammal and bird exhibits, animal hospital and T.rex bone yard.

Location: 455 N Galvin Pkwy, Phoenix, AZ 85008

Best Time to Visit: Summer to see animals enjoying the warmth

Fees: $39.95 adults, $29.95 kids 3-13, under 2 free

Directions: From Phoenix, west on Washington St, right on 7th Ave, right on I-10 E, exit AZ-202, exit Van Buren St, left on 52nd St, left on Van Buren St, left on Galvin Pkwy

GPS Coordinates: 33.4500°N, 111.9470°W

Nearest Town: Phoenix, about 20 minutes away

Interesting Facts: Formerly exhibited gorillas and snakes until dangerous incidents occurred in 1924.

South Mountain Park And Preserve

Why You Should Visit:

Hike over 50 miles of trails, camp at 150+ sites, and see panoramic views atop South Mountain at this vast city park. Enjoy the warmer weather far from the crowds.

Location: 10919 S Central Ave, Phoenix, AZ 85042

Best Time to Visit: Summer for ideal temperatures

Fees: Free admission

Directions: From Phoenix, west on Washington St, left on 7th Ave, left on Baseline Rd, right on Central Ave

GPS Coordinates: 33.3403°N, 112.0609°W

Nearest Town: Phoenix, about 15 minutes away

Interesting Facts: Popular 30-mile Alta Trail runs through, linking South Mountain with North Mountain.

The Duce

Why You Should Visit:

Savor Phoenix's lively nightlife at warehouse district spot The Duce. Grab a drink at its bars with live music, sing karaoke, or dance to a DJ. Check out the vintage clothing stores too!

Location: 525 S Central Ave, Phoenix, AZ 85004

Best Time to Visit: November-March for patio weather, or April-October for nightlife

Fees: No admission fee, individual vendor fees

Directions: From Phoenix, west on I-10, exit Grand Ave, right on Grand Ave, left on Monroe St, right on Central Ave

GPS Coordinates: 33.4423°N, 112.0732°W

Nearest Town: Tempe, about20 minutes away

Interesting Facts: Unique vintage clothing stores like Arcadia Trading and Ellie's.

PINE

Fossil Creek Dam

Why You Should Visit:

Look at this huge 900-foot travertine dam and ancient artifacts at Fossil Springs near Pine. Evidence of canal irrigation and past inhabitants offers a window into Arizona's history. Visitors can also opt to swim and wade in the pristine waters.

Location: Fossil Springs Wilderness, Pine, AZ 85544

Best Time to Visit: Spring and summer to see high water flows

Fees: Free, $4 dam viewing fee

Directions: From Pine, east on Hardscrabble Mesa Rd, left on AZ-260 W/AZ-87 N, left on Fossil Creek Rd W

GPS Coordinates: 34.4213°N, 111.5759°W

Nearest Town: Pine, about 25 minutes away

Interesting Facts: Featured on an episode of Ghost Adventures with reported paranormal activity.

Casa Grande Ruins

Native American Ruins

Why You Should Visit:

Explore the 1,000-year-old structures and artifacts left by the Quechan tribe at Casa Grande Ruins near Pine. See original walls, irrigation systems and dwellings for insights into ancient engineering and desert culture. **Location:** 31 Kokopeli Ln, Pine, AZ 85544

Best Time to Visit: Fall and winter for ideal peaceful conditions

Fees: Free admission

Directions: From Pine, east on Hardscrabble Mesa Rd, left on AZ-260 W, right on Anasazi Way, right on Ruin **Hill Loop**, left on Kokopeli Ln

GPS Coordinates: 34.3970°N, 111.4602°W

Nearest Town: Pine, about 10 minutes away

Interesting Facts: Arid climate kept the dwellings well preserved over time.

PRESCOTT

Courthouse Plaza

Why You Should Visit:

Enjoy public art, murals, sculptures and relaxing green space at Yavapai County Courthouse Plaza in Prescott. Don't miss the annual Mayfest celebration with vendors and live music.

Location: 120 S Cortez St, Prescott, AZ 86303

Best Time to Visit: Late May for the Mayfest festival

Fees: Free admission

Directions: From Prescott, south on E Goodwin St, right on S Cortez St

GPS Coordinates: 34°32'27.5064"N, 112°28'10.0992"W

Nearest Town: Prescott, about 5 minutes away

Interesting Facts: Built in 1873 as Arizona's first courthouse.

Watson Lake Park

Why You Should Visit:

Swim, fish, picnic and play at Watson Lake Park near Prescott. A former popular lake spot, it offers beautiful views and abundant wildlife.

Location: 3101 Watson Lake Park Rd, Prescott, AZ 86301

Best Time to Visit: Fall and winter for ideal conditions

Fees: $5 parking permit

Directions: From Prescott, south on E Goodwin St, left on S Pleasant St, right on E Gurley St, left on AZ-89 N, right on Watson Lake Park Rd

GPS Coordinates: 34°35'14.8848"N, 112°25'4.6956"W

Nearest Town: Prescott, about 10 minutes away

Interesting Facts: Said to be the ancestral home of the Yavapai people.

SCOTTSDALE

Arizona Boardwalk

Why You Should Visit:

Find endless things to do like shopping, dining, live music and games at Scottsdale Quarter. Don't miss the annual Water Bike Race and Air Show! This lively plaza entertains everyone.

Location: 9500 East Vía de Ventura, Scottsdale, AZ 85256

Best Time to Visit: February and March for big events

Fees: Free admission and parking

Directions: From Scottsdale, west on N Scottsdale Rd, right on E 3rd Ave, right on N Buckboard Trail, left on E Indian School Rd, left on AZ-101 Loop N, right on Via de Ventura

GPS Coordinates: 33.5553°N, 111.8769°W

Nearest Town: Scottsdale, about 15 minutes away

Interesting Facts: Built in 2005 as part of a $180 million downtown revitalization effort.

Butterfly Wonderland

Why You Should Visit:

See thousands of butterflies and exotic creatures at Butterfly Wonderland, featuring one of the country's largest indoor rainforest habitats. Don't miss the annual butterfly festival and exhibition.

Location: 9500 East Vía de Ventura F100, Scottsdale, AZ 85256

Best Time to Visit: April and May for the butterfly show

Fees: $22.95 adults, discounted rates

Directions: From Scottsdale, west on N Scottsdale Rd, right on E 3rd Ave, right on N Buckboard Trail, left on E Indian School Rd, left on AZ-101 Loop N, right on Via de Ventura

GPS Coordinates: 33.5545°N, 111.8762°W

Nearest Town: Scottsdale, about 10 minutes away

Interesting Facts: Recently renovated, doubling in size via a $14 million expansion.

Chaparral Park

(10)

Why You Should Visit:

Enjoy butterfly gardens, fishing, swimming, and outdoor concerts at Scottsdale's Eldorado Park. Don't miss the lively 3-week Fall Festival in the summer with crafts, food and performances.

Location: 7642 E Redfield Rd, Scottsdale, AZ 85254

Best Time to Visit: Summer for the Fall Festival

Fees: $2 parking fee

Directions: From Scottsdale, west on N Scottsdale Rd, right on E Camelback Rd, left on N Hayden Rd, right on E Jackrabbit Rd

GPS Coordinates: 33.5154°N, 111.9072°W

Nearest Town: Scottsdale, about 10 minutes away

Interesting Facts: Home of the Scottsdale Philharmonic Orchestra, with concerts year-round.

Frank Lloyd Wright Spire

Why You Should Visit:

Let be inspired by architect Frank Lloyd Wright's slender 2,427-foot concrete and glass spire, featuring views from the top platform. Learn about its design and construction at this architectural landmark.

Location: 7207 E Frank Lloyd Wright Blvd, Scottsdale, AZ 85260

Best Time to Visit: Winter for smaller crowds and mild weather

Fees: $22 adults, discounted rates

Directions: From Scottsdale, west on N Scottsdale Rd, right on E Frank Lloyd Wright Blvd

GPS Coordinates: 33.6377°N, 111.9249°W

Nearest Town: Scottsdale, about 15-18 minutes away

Interesting Facts: Based on St. Paul's Cathedral in London with a spiral ramp inside.

Huhugam Ki Museum

Why You Should Visit:

See expansive Native American exhibits and artifacts at Scottsdale Museum of the West. Don't miss the lively Grand Opening festival each summer showcasing tribal culture.

Location: 10005 E Osborn Rd, Scottsdale, AZ 85256

Best Time to Visit: Summer for the Grand Opening event

Fees: $4 parking fee

Directions: From Scottsdale, west on N Scottsdale Rd, right on E 3rd Ave, right on N Buckboard Trail, left on E Indian School Rd, right on N Longmore Rd

GPS Coordinates: 33.4871°N, 111.8648°W

Nearest Town: Scottsdale, about 10 minutes away

Interesting Facts: Gift shop sells Native American handicrafts. The onsite restaurant features Indian cuisine.

Macdonal's Ranch

Why You Should Visit:

Hike scenic trails, ride horses, bike, fish and see wildlife at MacDonald's Ranch. With varied terrain and great views, this historic ranch offers numerous outdoor adventures.

Location: 26540 N Scottsdale Rd, Scottsdale, AZ 85255

Best Time to Visit: October-March for nice weather

Fees: $10 adults, discounted rates

Directions: From Scottsdale, west on McKellips Rd, left on Miller Rd, right on Rancho Vista Dr, right on Redfield Rd, left on Reems Rd, right on Scottsdale Rd, left on Reems Rd, right on Scottsdale Rd

GPS Coordinates: 33.7242°N, 111.9255°W

Nearest Town: Phoenix, about 30 minutes away

Interesting Facts: Originally owned by Thomas T. Macdonald in 1885.

Mccormick-Stillman Railroad Park

Why You Should Visit:

Train lovers of all ages should visit McCormick-Stillman Railroad Park. Ride the 15" gauge railroad, see model trains, tour the museum, or walk through the vintage railcars. With so much railroad history and action, it's a one-of-a-kind attraction.

Location: 7301 E Indian Bend Rd, Scottsdale, AZ 85250

Best Time to Visit: October to March for ideal weather

Fees: No entrance fee, $3 per ride

Directions: From Scottsdale, west on N Scottsdale Rd, right on E Indian Bend Rd

GPS Coordinates: 33.5371°N, 111.9233°W

Nearest Town: Scottsdale, about 10 minutes away

Interesting Facts: Founded in 1962 by Mike McCormick and Don Stillman. Has functioning vintage trolleys and streetcars.

Mcdowell Sonoran Preserve

Why You Should Visit:

Gateway Trailhead in the McDowell Sonoran Preserve offers nature lovers an oasis minutes from Scottsdale. Birdwatchers can spot wildlife along miles of trails winding through this peaceful desert landscape. With its abundance of flora and fauna, it's a great spot for escaping urban life.

Location: 18333 N Thompson Peak Pkwy, Scottsdale, AZ 85255

Best Time to Visit: Fall and winter for ideal conditions

Fees: Free admission

Directions: From Scottsdale, west on N Scottsdale Rd, right on E 3rd Ave,

right on Buckboard Trail, left on E Indian School Rd, left on AZ-101 Loop N, right on N Thompson Peak Pkwy

GPS Coordinates: 33.6494°N, 111.8585°W

Nearest Town: Scottsdale, about 20 minutes away

Interesting Facts: Part of the 28,000 acre Tonto National Forest.

Octane Raceway

Why You Should Visit:

Get your adrenaline pumping at Octane Raceway in Scottsdale. With go-karts, water slides, driving courses and events, this action-packed spot promises adventure for all ages.

Location: 9119 Talking Stick Way, Scottsdale, AZ 85250

Best Time to Visit: November through February for nice weather

Fees: Vary by activity

Directions: From Scottsdale, west on N Scottsdale Rd, right on E 3rd Ave, right on Buckboard Trail, left on E Indian School Rd, left on AZ-101 Loop N, right on Talking Stick Way

GPS Coordinates: 33.5360°N, 111.8846°W

Nearest Town: Scottsdale, about 15 minutes away

Interesting Facts: Originally opened as Redington Motorsports Park, founded by Jerome Mack.

Odysea Aquarium

Why You Should Visit:

See over 120 exotic fish species in one of Arizona's largest aquariums at OdySea in Scottsdale. Feed sharks, take a boat tour, or snorkel - this marine world offers interactive family fun.

Location: 9500 E Vía de Ventura Suite A-100, Scottsdale, AZ 85256

Best Time to Visit: May through October

Fees: $41.95 adults, $31.95 ages 2-12, under 2 free

Directions: From Scottsdale, west on N Scottsdale Rd, right on E 3rd Ave, right on Buckboard Trail, left on E Indian School Rd, left on AZ-101 Loop N, right on Via de Ventura

GPS Coordinates: 33.5884°N, 111.9217°W

Nearest Town: Scottsdale, about 15 minutes away

Interesting Facts: Formerly known as Maricopa County Aquarium, founded over 60 years ago.

Old Town Scottsdale

Why You Should Visit:

Old Town Scottsdale invites strolls down lively pedestrian streets lined with art galleries, restaurants, and historic buildings. Soak up the vibe of this district that has been a hub of activity in Arizona since the 1880s. Old Town offers a fun glimpse into the state's past.

Location: Old Town Scottsdale, Scottsdale, AZ 85251

Best Time to Visit: May through October for nice weather

Fees: Free admission

Directions: From Scottsdale, west on N Scottsdale Rd

GPS Coordinates: 33.4984°N, 111.9261°W

Nearest Town: Scottsdale, minutes away

Interesting Facts: Once called Goodyear Heights before Goodyear Tire moved in. Nicknamed "Valley of the Sun."

Pinnacle Peak Park

Why You Should Visit:

Hike scenic trails with panoramic views and bring your leashed pets to Pinnacle Peak Park near Scottsdale. The popular but short hike up Pinnacle Peak offers beautiful vistas. Follow park rules to keep pets safe on the steep, cliff-lined trails.

Location: 26802 N 102nd Way, Scottsdale, AZ 85262

Best Time to Visit: March to November for ideal weather

Fees: Free admission

Directions: From Scottsdale, west on N Scottsdale Rd, right on E 3rd Ave, right on Buckboard Trail, left on Indian School Rd, left on AZ-101 Loop N, right on Pima Rd, right on Happy Valley Rd, left on Alma School Rd, left on Pinnacle Peak Pkwy, straight on 102nd Way

GPS Coordinates: 33.7279°N, 111.8604°W

Nearest Town: Scottsdale, about 35 minutes away

Interesting Facts: The peak's springs were used by Native Americans for celebrations and healing.

Scottsdale Museum Of Contemporary Art

Why You Should Visit:

See diverse, ever-changing art exhibits at the Scottsdale Museum of Contemporary Art. Sculptures, photos, performances - with new installations annually, there's always something fresh.

Location: 7374 E 2nd St, Scottsdale, AZ 85251

Best Time to Visit: March-May for special events

Fees: $10 online, $12 at door. Discounts available.

Directions: From Scottsdale, west on N Scottsdale Rd, right on E 3rd Ave, right on Drinkwater Blvd, right on E 2nd St, right on Wells Fargo Ave

GPS Coordinates: 33.4916°N, 111.9229°W

Nearest Town: Scottsdale, about 5 minutes away

Interesting Facts: Designed by the famous architect Frank Lloyd Wright.

Scottsdale Xeriscape Garden

Why You Should Visit:

See sustainable gardening shine at Scottsdale Xeriscape Garden, where talented horticulturists arranged innovative dry climate plants. Gardeners, take a peaceful stroll through the creatively designed spaces that highlight water conservation in the desert. It's a great spot to get xeriscape inspiration!

Location: 5401 N Hayden Rd, Scottsdale, AZ 85250

Best Time to Visit: Spring and summer for ideal flower viewing

Fees: Free admission, $5 parking

Directions: From Scottsdale, west on N Scottsdale Rd, right on E Camelback Rd, left on N Hayden Rd, right on E Starlight Way

GPS Coordinates: 33.5212°N, 111.9074°W

Nearest Town: Scottsdale, about 10 minutes away

Interesting Facts: Formerly the site of the Scottsdale Arabian Horse Show before becoming a public garden.

Sereno Park

Why You Should Visit:

Seek peace and tranquility surrounded by nature at Chaparral Park in Scottsdale. Stroll or walk dogs along lush trails and lakes at this oasis offering a reprieve from city life.

Location: 5720 E Sweetwater Ave, Scottsdale, AZ 85254

Best Time to Visit: Spring and summer to see blooms

Fees: Free admission

Directions: From Scottsdale, west on N Scottsdale Rd, right on E Cactus Rd, right on N 56th St

GPS Coordinates: 33.6061°N, 111.9584°W

Nearest Town: Scottsdale, about 20 minutes away

Interesting Facts: Offers pristine mountain views overlooking the city of Scottsdale.

Soleri Bridge

(11)

Why You Should Visit:

See Paolo Soleri's stunning glass pedestrian bridge over the Salt River at Soleri Bridge Park in Scottsdale. Offering beautiful city views, it's a work of art and a great photo spot.

Location: 4420 N Scottsdale Rd, Scottsdale, AZ 85251

Best Time to Visit: Summer for ideal weather

Fees: Free admission

Directions: From Scottsdale, west on N Scottsdale Rd

GPS Coordinates: 33.8165°N, 112.4203°W

Nearest Town: Scottsdale, about 5 minutes away

Interesting Facts: Bridge architecture is described as a "temple of glass."

Sunrise Peak

Why You Should Visit:

For an incredible bucket list experience, hike up Scottsdale's Sunrise Peak early to catch breathtaking city views at 2650 ft. Watch the city wake up from above on this peaceful hike before the crowds arrive. It's a view that shouldn't be missed!

Location: Sunrise Peak, Scottsdale, AZ 85259

Best Time to Visit: Weekdays for smaller crowds

Fees: Free admission

Directions: From Scottsdale, west on N Scottsdale Rd, right on E 3rd Ave, right on Buckboard Trail, left on Indian School Rd, left on AZ-101 Loop N, right on Shea Blvd, left on 136th St, left on Sweetwater Ave, left on 137th St

GPS Coordinates: 33.9556°N, 109.5590°W

Nearest Town: Scottsdale, about 30 minutes away

Interesting Facts: Quieter on weekends or evenings than busy weekday mornings.

Taliesin West

Why You Should Visit:

Tour the desert home and studio of architect Frank Lloyd Wright at Taliesin West in Scottsdale. Though the house is closed, see the grounds, studio, furniture and more at this National Historic Landmark Wright designed and lived in.

Location: 12621 N Frank Lloyd Wright Blvd, Scottsdale, AZ 85259

Best Time to Visit: Winter for ideal weather

Fees: $49 adults, discounted rates

Directions: From Scottsdale, west on N Scottsdale Rd, right on E 3rd Ave, right on Buckboard Trail, left on Indian School Rd, left on AZ-101 Loop N, exit Cactus Rd, straight on Taliesin Dr

GPS Coordinates: 33.6064°N, 111.8452°W

Nearest Town: Scottsdale, about 25 minutes away

Interesting Facts: One of Wright's first projects after returning from Japan, inspired by Japanese architecture.

Wonderspaces Arizona

Why You Should Visit:

Spark creativity and imagination at WonderSpaces in Scottsdale. Interactive music, art and science exhibits designed by local artists encourage innovation for all ages. Don't miss the monthly "Art Through the Ages" exhibition.

Location: 7014 E Camelback Rd #584, Scottsdale, AZ 85251

Best Time to Visit: Summer for the special art exhibition

Fees: $22 adults and kids 4-12

Directions: From Scottsdale, west on N Scottsdale Rd, left on E Camelback Rd, right on N Goldwater Blvd

GPS Coordinates: 33°54'9.7904"N, 111°52'15.1136"W

Nearest Town: Scottsdale, about 5 minutes away

Interesting Facts: Part of a chain conceived by Jeff Jackson when his kids made an art gallery in their garage.

SEDONA

Amitabha Stupa And Peace Park

Why You Should Visit:

Find relaxation surrounded by nature at Amitabha Stupa & Peace Park in Sedona. Enjoy the pool, Buddha statues, fountain, meditation events, and summer art shows at this tranquil oasis.

Location: 2650 Pueblo Dr, Sedona, AZ 86336

Best Time to Visit: Summer for special events

Fees: $2 parking fee, donations accepted

Directions: From Sedona, south on State Route 89A, exit AZ-89A W, right on Andante Dr, left on Pueblo Dr, right on Stupa

GPS Coordinates: 34.8756°N, 111.8083°W

Nearest Town: Sedona, about 10 minutes away

Interesting Facts: Home to the Sedona Center for Spiritual Living which hosts retreats and classes. Also features a lush garden.

Bell Rock

Why You Should Visit:

Bell Rock's majestic red rock formation is a must-see near Sedona. This iconic sandstone hoodoo is perfect for hiking, rock climbing, biking, or fossil hunting while surrounded by awe-inspiring desert views. Its unique shape stands out dramatically against the landscape. Whether you're up for adventure or just want to marvel at natural beauty and capture incredible photos, Bell Rock has something for everyone.

Location: 4999 State Route 179, Sedona, AZ 86351

Best Time to Visit: November-March for ideal conditions

Fees: $3 daily hiking pass

Directions: From Sedona, north on State Route 179

GPS Coordinates: 34.2491°N, -111.4151°W

Nearest Town: Sedona, about 15 minutes away

Interesting Facts: Surrounded by a Native American legend about a man named Tso who refused to move his home.

Slide Rock State Park

Why You Should Visit:

Escape the heat at Slide Rock State Park, where you can slide down the famous natural water chute or soak in Oak Creek's refreshing waters surrounded by stunning red rock views. The scenic hiking trails showcase the area's natural beauty. Perfect for families looking to cool off while admiring the gorgeous high-desert landscape of Arizona.

Location: 6871 AZ-89A, Sedona, AZ 86336

Best Time to Visit: November-March to avoid summer heat

Fees: $5-$15 for slide and hot spring access

Directions: From Sedona, west on AZ-89A

GPS Coordinates: 34.9436°N, 111.7529°W

Nearest Town: Sedona, about 15 minutes away

Interesting Facts: Formed by erosion of swampy Oak Creek over time.

Chapel Of The Holy Cross

Why You Should Visit:

See the striking Catholic church built into the red rock cliffs at the Chapel of the Holy Cross in Sedona. Even non-Catholics will appreciate the breathtaking views, trails, and picnicking at this scenic state park.

Location: 780 Chapel Rd, Sedona, AZ 86336

Best Time to Visit: April-October for blooms, or November-March for ideal photos

Fees: Free admission

Directions: From Sedona, north on AZ-179, left on US-89A, right on Chapel Rd

GPS Coordinates: 34.8320°N, 111.7668°W

Nearest Town: Sedona, about 15 minutes away

Interesting Facts: Built in the 1950s with Italian architecture similar to the Vatican. Stained glass windows made in Italy.

Red Rock State Park

Why You Should Visit:

Surrounded by awe-inspiring red rock formations, Arizona's renowned Red Rock State Park entices outdoor adventurers with activities like hiking forested trails, rock climbing, and zip lining. Cool off in the crystal-clear pools or simply admire the breathtaking scenery. With stunning natural beauty and ample recreation, this remarkable park has something for everyone to enjoy.

Location: 4050 Red Rock Loop Rd, Sedona, AZ 86336

Best Time to Visit: May-September for warm weather, or October-April for fall colors

Fees: $7 ages 14+, $4 ages 7-13, and under 6 free

Directions: From Sedona, south on AZ-89A, exit AZ-89A W, left on Red Rock Loop Rd

GPS Coordinates: 34.8129°N, 111.8306°W

Nearest Town: Sedona, about 20 minutes away

Interesting Facts: Officially named in 1982 after being founded in 1968 to preserve the wilderness.

Sedona Performing Arts Center

Why You Should Visit:

Catch a show, musical or concert at Sedona's state-of-the-art Performing Arts Center. Home of the Sedona Film Festival, this 1,300 seat theater hosts diverse events and performances.

Location: 995 Upper Red Rock Loop Rd, Sedona, AZ 86336

Best Time to Visit: April-September for ideal weather

Fees: Average $131 per ticket

Directions: From Sedona, south on AZ-89A, exit AZ-89A W, left on Upper Red Rock Loop Rd, right on Stadium Dr

GPS Coordinates: 34.8468°N, 111.8306°W

Nearest Town: Sedona, about 10 minutes away

Interesting Facts: Opened in 2011, it's the only performing arts center within 200 miles and has the most seats in northern Arizona.

Snoopy Rock

(12)

Why You Should Visit:

The kids will get a kick out of Snoopy Rock near Sedona, where trails wind past whimsical rocks shaped like Snoopy and Woodstock! Enjoy the playground, waterfall views, and searching for more Peanuts gang "characters" in the rocks. It's a scenic spot families will love.

Location: Snoopy Rock, Sedona, AZ 86336

Best Time to Visit: Spring and fall for ideal rock shapes and water flow

Fees: $5 admission, $2 parking

Directions: From Sedona, south on AZ-89A, exit AZ-179 S, exit Schnebly Hill Rd, west on Rosabelle Rd, left on McClintock Dr

GPS Coordinates: 34.8603°N, 111.7516°W

Nearest Town: Sedona, about 5 minutes away

Interesting Facts: Home to a 2.5 mile out and back hiking trail. Bring snacks to attract birds!

Tlaquepaque Arts And Crafts Village

Why You Should Visit:

Shop, dine and see art from around the world at Tlaquepaque Arts Village in Sedona. With over 40 galleries in an authentic Mexican-style layout, it's a top spot to buy quality artisan goods.

Location: 336 AZ-179, Sedona, AZ 86336

Best Time to Visit: April-September for nice weather

Fees: Free admission, fees for purchases

Directions: From Sedona, south on AZ-89A, exit AZ-179 S, left on Forest Rd 10A

GPS Coordinates: 34°51'43.9236"N, 111°45'47.3148"W

Nearest Town: Sedona, about 5 minutes away

Interesting Facts: Founded in 1972 and modeled after a traditional Mexican village, celebrating local arts.

Rio Salado Habitat

Why You Should Visit:

Hike, bike, birdwatch and explore the woods and wetlands at Tempe's Rio Salado Habitat. With lush vegetation and abundant wildlife, it's a natural oasis minutes from downtown.

Location: 525 E Gilbert Dr, Tempe, AZ 85281

Best Time to Visit: Spring and summer for blooms

Fees: Free admission

Directions: From Tempe, north on Mill Ave, right on Curry Rd, right on College Ave, left on Gilbert Dr

GPS Coordinates: 33.5488°N, 112.1658°W

Nearest Town: Tempe, about 10 minutes away

Interesting Facts: Named for owner Lopiano Panero who helped restore and maintain the area.

TEMPE

Legoland Discovery Center Arizona

Why You Should Visit:

At Legoland Discovery Center in Tempe, kids of all ages can explore interactive Lego exhibits, rides, shows and more. With over 3 million Legos on display, it's the world's largest Legoland!

Location: 5000 S Arizona Mills Cir STE 135, Tempe, AZ 85282

Best Time to Visit: Holidays for special Lego events

Fees: $28.99 per person

Directions: From Tempe, west on 5th St, left on Farmer Ave, right after Chili's, left on Priest Dr, right on Arizona Mills Cir

GPS Coordinates: 33.5619°N, 112.1569°W

Nearest Town: Tempe, about 15 minutes away

Interesting Facts: Home to multiple exhibits and shows with life-sized Lego character actors.

Lopiano Bosque Habitat

Why You Should Visit:

Outdoor enthusiasts should visit Lopiano Bosque Habitat in Tempe to hike, bike, and birdwatch through 13 acres of lush woods and wetlands. With abundant wildlife and native plants, it's a peaceful natural escape minutes from the city. Blooming flowers make spring and summer ideal, but the habitat impresses year-round. This nature area was restored in 2000 by local owner Lopiano Panero, who continues to support its upkeep. Wandering the trails is a great way to unwind and get back to nature without leaving town.

Location: 525 E Gilbert Dr, Tempe, AZ 85281

Best Time to Visit: Spring and summer for flowers, or anytime

Fees: Free admission

Directions: From Tempe, north on Mill Ave, right on Curry Rd, right on College Ave, left on Gilbert Dr

GPS: 33.5488°N, 112.1658°W

Nearest Town: Tempe, about 10 minutes away

Interesting Facts: Named for owner Lopiano Panero who helped restore and maintain the area.

Rio Salado Park

Why You Should Visit:

Exercise, unwind, and see shows at Rio Salado Park. Stroll the paths, admire the scenic views, and catch a performance at the lakefront amphitheater.
Location: 80 W Rio Salado Pkwy, Tempe, AZ 85281

Best Time to Visit: Sunrise or sunset for ideal lighting

Fees: $2 parking, donations accepted

Directions: From Tempe, north on Mill Ave, left on Rio Salado Pkwy

GPS Coordinates: 33.4312°N, 111.9410°W

Nearest Town: Tempe, about 5 minutes away

Interesting Facts: Part of Rio Salado Park, home to skiing, fishing and boating activities.

Tempe Beach Park

Why You Should Visit:

Gather a group and enjoy Tempe Beach Park's scenic water features like slides, dog parks and even concerts. With amenities for pets and kids, it's a lively spot for soaking up sunshine and summer events.

Location: 80 W Rio Salado Pkwy, Tempe, AZ 85281

Best Time to Visit: Summer for ideal weather and entertainment

Fees: $2 parking fee

Directions: From Tempe, west on 5th St, right on Ash Ave, straight on Rio Salado Pkwy

GPS Coordinates: 33.4318°N, 111.9426°W

Nearest Town: Tempe, about 5 minutes away

Interesting Facts: Home to family events like bingo and karaoke. Has full-size bathrooms with baby changing stations.

TUCSON

Arizona-Sonora Desert Museum

Why You Should Visit:

See over 1,900 plant and animal species from around the world at Arizona-Sonora Desert Museum near Tucson. Learn about geology, astronomy and more through indoor/outdoor exhibits and amphitheaters.

Location: 2021 N Kinney Rd, Tucson, AZ 85743

Best Time to Visit: October-November for Native American cultural events

Fees: $29.95 adults, discounted rates

Directions: From Tucson, west on Jacinto St, left on Oracle Rd, right on Grant Rd, right on Freeway, left on I-10 W, exit Cortaro Rd, right on Cortaro Rd, right on Silverbell Rd, right on Cantora Way

GPS Coordinates: 32.2440°N, 111.1682°W

Nearest Town: Tucson, about 20 minutes away

Interesting Facts: Located on a former 60-acre goat ranch, donated to the UofA in the 1970s.

Catalina State Park

Catalina State Park

Why You Should Visit:

Catalina State Park's gorgeous scenery and terrain make it a paradise for outdoor adventures. Hike through canyons and washes, cast for trout and bass in the lake, pitch a tent at the campground, or cool off with a swim. With desert views and abundant wildlife sightings, this beloved park near

Tucson offers the quintessential nature escape to experience Arizona's natural splendor.

Location: 11570 N Oracle Rd, Tucson, AZ 85737

Best Time to Visit: November-March for ideal weather

Fees: No entrance fee, camping and activity fees apply

Directions: From Tucson, southwest on Ajo Way, right on Palo Verde Rd, left on Rita Rd, right on Camp Lowell Rd, left on Camino De Oeste Ln, right on Camino Del Cerro

GPS Coordinates: 32.4364°N, 110.9096°W

Nearest Town: Tucson, about 25 minutes away

Interesting Facts: Named after a former nearby mountain known for its beauty.

El Presidio Historic Distric

Why You Should Visit:

Explore the history of Spanish missions and military life at Tucson's El Presidio Historic District. Murals and artifacts offer insights into the people and cultures that once thrived here.

Location: El Presidio Historic District, Tucson, AZ 85701

Best Time to Visit: Year-round

Fees: $3 admission

Directions: From Tucson, west on Jacinto St, left on Oracle Rd, left on Main Ave, left on Granada Ave, left on 6th St, right on Main Ave

GPS Coordinates: 32.19520°N, 110.981081°W

Nearest Town: Tucson, about 10 minutes away

Interesting Facts: Named after the Tepi Oki tribe, meaning "sun people" in the O'odham language.

Fort Lowell Park

Why You Should Visit:

History buffs should check out Fort Lowell Park's 700 acres of 19th century buildings and artifacts near Tucson. Play mini golf, see riverboats and military relics, and catch events like the Zuni Food & Family Festival.

Location: 2900 N. Craycroft Rd. Tucson, AZ 85712

Best Time to Visit: April-October for festivals like Zuni Food & Family

Fees: $10 covers activities

Directions: From Tucson, east on Jacinto St, right on Stone Ave, left on Grant Rd, left on Craycroft Rd

GPS Coordinates: 32.2597°N, 110.8747°W

Nearest Town: Tucson, about 20 minutes away

Interesting Facts: Established in 1874 as a military camp for 15,000+ Union soldiers.

International Wildlife Museum

Why You Should Visit:

Get an up-close look at 400+ lifelike animal exhibits at the creative and educational International Wildlife Museum near Tucson. Special programs let you interact with animals and appreciate nature.

Location: 4800 West Gates Pass, Boulevard, Tucson, AZ 85745

Best Time to Visit: March-May for ideal weather

Fees: $10 adults, discounted rates

Directions: From Tucson, west on Jacinto St, left on Oracle Rd, right on Grant Rd, left on Ironwood Hill Dr, left on Camino De Oeste, right on Gates Pass Rd

GPS Coordinates: 32.2346°N, 111.0671°W

Nearest Town: Tucson, about 15 minutes away

Interesting Facts: Originally built in 1963, with major renovations in 1977 and 1983 to improve exhibits.

Mission San Xavier Del Bac

(13)

Why You Should Visit:

Explore original 17th century Spanish mission buildings and stunning grounds at Mission San Xavier del Bac near Tucson. Murals and a museum detail the mission's 300-year history in the region.

Location: 1950 W San Xavier Rd, Tucson, AZ 85746

Best Time to Visit: April-June, September-November for ideal weather

Fees: Free admission

Directions: From Tucson, west on Jacinto St, left on Oracle Rd, right on Speedway Blvd, left on I-10 E, exit I-19 S, exit San Xavier Rd, right on San Xavier Rd, right on Little Nogales Dr

GPS Coordinates: 32.1070°N, 111.0088°W

Nearest Town: Tucson, about 20 minutes away

Interesting Facts: Named for the mission founded here by Spanish friars in 1692 near Tucson.

Prima Air & Space Museum

Why You Should Visit:

See aircraft, rockets, satellites and more at Pima Air & Space Museum near Tucson. Learn about aviation history or experience an immersive flight simulation ride. Great for aspiring astronauts!

Location: 6000 E Valencia Rd, Tucson, AZ 85756

Best Time to Visit: Spring, summer or fall

Fees: $19.50 adults, discounted rates

Directions: From Tucson, west on Jacinto St, left on Oracle Rd, right on Speedway Blvd, left on I-10 E, exit Valencia Rd, left on Valencia Rd

GPS Coordinates: 32.2384°N, 110.9156°W

Nearest Town: Tucson, about 20 minutes away

Interesting Facts: Offers a 4-5 minute flight simulation ride for $10 per person

Reid Park Zoo

Why You Should Visit:

Get up close to elephants, giraffes, monkeys and more at this lively Tucson zoo. It's fun for the whole family to see incredible wildlife in engaging natural habitats. Don't miss the playful otters, colorful flamingos, and silly penguins!

Location: 3400 E Zoo Ct, Tucson, AZ 85716

Best Time to Visit: October to May to avoid extreme heat

Fees: $10.50 adults, discounts for seniors and kids

Directions: From Tucson, east on Broadway Blvd, left on 22nd St, left on Zoo Ct

GPS Coordinates: 32.2099°N, 110.9207°W

Nearest Town: Tucson, about a 10-15 minute drive

Interesting Facts: Established in 1927 as the Tucson Zoological Gardens

Trail Dust Town

Why You Should Visit:

Saddle up for some family fun at Trail Dust Town, an authentic 1880s frontier town created just for kicks. Catch live stunt shows, ride the train, and shop and dine Old West-style. It's a rootin' tootin' good time for anyone who digs the Wild West!

Location: 6541 E Tanque Verde Rd, Tucson, AZ 85715

Best Time to Visit: Spring or fall for pleasant weather

Fees: Free entry, $5 for train rides

Directions: From Tucson, east on Grant Rd, right on Tanque Verde Rd

GPS Coordinates: 32.2474°N, 110.8529°W

Nearest Town: Tucson, around 15 minutes away

Interesting Facts: Site of films like The Good, The Bad and The Ugly

Tucson Botanical Gardens

Why You Should Visit:

Stroll along curving paths past colorful native plants and flowers that attract fluttering butterflies. Pick a shady spot for a relaxing picnic or just find a bench and unwind surrounded by these lush gardens. With gorgeous scenery and a peaceful ambience, it's the perfect place to rejuvenate.

Location: 700 N. Kinney Rd, Tucson, AZ 85743

Best Time to Visit: Spring or fall when blooms peak

Fees: $15 adults, discounts available

Directions: From Tucson, east on Grant Rd, right on Alvernon Way

GPS Coordinates: 32.2485°N, 110.9088°W

Nearest Town: Tucson, around a 10 minute drive

Interesting Facts: Home to a native plant conservation society

Tumamoc Hill

Why You Should Visit:

Climb Tumamoc Hill for amazing views and a window into Tucson's ancient past. Check out centuries-old petroglyphs, dig for artifacts, and learn about the area's original native people. When the sun sets, appreciate epic stargazing from this peaceful spot steeped in history.

Location: Tumamoc Hill Rd, Tucson, AZ 85730

Best Time to Visit: Evening when temperatures cool down

Fees: Free entry, $3 for guided tours

Directions: From Tucson, west on St Mary's Rd, left on Anklam Rd, right on Tumamoc Hill Rd

GPS Coordinates: 32.2255°N, 111.0016°W

Nearest Town: Tucson, around a 10-15 minute drive

Interesting Facts: Formerly known as Old Spanish Trail Hill, part of a trade route

TOMBSTONE

Bird Cage Theater

Why You Should Visit:

Experience the Old West at Tombstone's historic Bird Cage Theater, filled with artifacts and mementos transporting you back in time. Marvel at the legendary barber chair and antiques while picturing the theater's lively past. This one-of-a-kind attraction offers an engaging glimpse into frontier history.

Location: 535 E Allen St, Tombstone, AZ 85638

Best Time to Visit: October or November for special events

Fees: $12-$14 entry, parking fee

Directions: From downtown Tombstone, head north on 4th St, right on Fremont, right on 6th St

GPS Coordinates: 31.7119°N, 110.0652°W

Nearest Town: Tombstone, 1-5 minutes away

Interesting Facts: Site of classic Western films with authentic bullet holes

O.k. Corral

Why You Should Visit:

Transport back to the Wild West at the legendary O.K. Corral in Tombstone, home to outdoor exhibits and original buildings. Walk in the footsteps of frontier legends like the Earps and the Clantons who battled here in 1881. Relive an intriguing era of American history.

Location: 326 E Allen St, Tombstone, AZ 85638

Best Time to Visit: October or November for special events

Fees: $6 entry, free under 5, parking fee

Directions: From downtown Tombstone, head north on 4th St, right on Fremont, left on 6th St

GPS Coordinates: 31.7130°N, 110.0676°W

Nearest Town: Tombstone, 1-5 minutes away

Interesting Facts: Designated an official Arizona state historical park in 1971

TUSAYAN

Grand Canyon National Park

(14)

Why You Should Visit:

Marvel at the breathtaking views and natural beauty of the iconic Grand Canyon, carved over millions of years. As you stand on the rim and gaze out at the immense gorge, you'll be awestruck by the sheer scale and drama of this natural wonder. Descend into the canyon on winding trails to see rock layers unveiling the earth's geological history. Watch the setting sun cast a glow on the ancient, sculpted walls. The Grand Canyon's stunning vistas and timeless presence make it a bucket list destination.

Location: Grand Canyon National Park, Arizona 86023

Best Time to Visit: July-September during the dry season

Fees: $35 per vehicle

Directions: From Tusayan, west on Hwy 64, right on 64/331/661 into the park

GPS Coordinates: 36.2679°N, 112.3535°W

Nearest Town: Tusayan, 2-5 minutes away

Interesting Facts: More than 2.3 miles deep, one of the most impressive canyons in the world

WINSLOW

Meteor Crater Natural Landmark

Why You Should Visit:

See the breathtaking Meteor Crater Natural Landmark, a massive 550-foot deep impact crater formed 50,000 years ago when a meteorite struck the Arizona desert. Marvel at the sheer size and scope of this extraterrestrial wonder as you walk along the rim. Discover how scientists study its geology to unlock secrets about asteroid collisions and our solar system's past. This otherworldly site offers a fascinating glimpse into an ancient cosmic event.

Location: Interstate 40, Exit 233, Winslow, AZ 86047

Best Time to Visit: May through October for ideal weather

Fees: $25 adults, discounted rates

Directions: From Winslow, west on I-40, take Exit 233 for Meteor Crater Rd

GPS Coordinates: 35.0278°N, 111.0222°W

Nearest Town: Winslow, about 30 minutes away

Interesting Facts: Nearly 1,200 feet deep and 4,000 feet wide. An important geologic site.

Arizona Itineraries And Trips Proposals

(15)

Into the Gran Canyon State Itinerary

Cruise through Arizona's jaw-dropping landscapes on this 7-day driving tour. From cactus-dotted deserts to pine-topped mountains, soak up the diverse beauty and old-west spirit of the Grand Canyon State.

Day 1 - Tucson to Tombstone

Kick things off in cultural Tucson before hitting the road through Saguaro Country to the historic town of Tombstone. Walk the same dusty streets as old west cowboys and experience frontier life at sites like the O.K. Corral. Chow down on comfort grub at the Bird Cage Theater, now a restaurant with retro flair.

111

Day 2 - Tombstone to Phoenix

Venture through cactus-laden desert from Tombstone to Phoenix, founded in 1868 and once the 8th biggest US city. Learn about Native American art and culture at the renowned Heard Museum's galleries and exhibits. Glimpse into Arizona's future at the Arizona Science Center's innovative science displays. When the sun sets, unwind in style at The Duce's lively warehouse district, sampling Phoenix's nightlife scene all in one spot through its hoppin' restaurant, retro bar, music and games.

Day 3 - Phoenix to Sedona

Meander from Phoenix up through the red rocks to Sedona, a haven for artists and creatives drawn by its natural beauty and spiritual energy. Cool off sliding down natural waterslides at Slide Rock State Park, popular for its thrilling 60-foot slick rock slides. Find zen at the Chapel of the Holy Cross, considered a spiritual vortex for its peaceful, uplifting energy. Fuel up on local flavor at Sedona's artsy cafes and restaurants before calling it a night.

Day 4 - Explore Sedona

Start your day ascending Red Rock State Park before sunrise, taking in epic views of the surrounding red rock country. Afterward, browse the boutiques, galleries and eateries at Tlaquepaque Arts and Crafts Village. When the sun dips low, tap into the nightlife at local bars, then cap it off stargazing along Red Rock Loop Trail, watching for meteors.

Day 5 - Sedona to Flagstaff

Make tracks from Sedona's red rocks up to Flagstaff, nestled in a picturesque valley beneath the soaring San Francisco Peaks. Called an outdoor mecca, hike the volcanic cinder trails of extinct Sunset Crater Volcano, which erupted just 300 years back. After exploring lava flows and volcanic scenery, kick back with friendly locals over craft brews at Flagstaff's lively watering holes.

Day 6 - Explore Flagstaff

Spend the morning at Lowell Observatory, where astronomer Percival Lowell pioneered stellar research. Tour the historic site and gaze at galaxies through its vintage telescopes. Then explore Flagstaff's funky downtown, browsing kitschy shops and drinking in the city's musical legacy at local bars. Keep an ear out for the rhythms and melodies that inspired famous tunes penned here.

Day 7 - Rest and Go Home

After a week of Arizona adventuring, take a day to recharge before pointing the car homeward. This epic road trip teaches you to live in the moment and appreciate the journey. You'll gain knowledge of Arizona's culture and unforgettable landscapes. Heading home, remember to plan ahead - pack pet supplies, medications, phone chargers and more. Most of all, drive safely after this once-in-a-lifetime Grand Canyon State getaway.

Arizona's Highlights In 1 Week

This action-packed 7-day itinerary hits Arizona's top sights for first-timers. See the main attractions and get a taste of the Grand Canyon State on a tight schedule and budget.

Day 1 - Phoenix:

Kick off your Arizona adventure in Phoenix. Hike up iconic Camelback Mountain for stunning city views from its scenic trails. At sunset, wander Desert Botanical Garden's one-of-a-kind cactus and succulent collection, featuring rare species found only in Arizona. Rest up for more excitement ahead.

Day 2 - Explore Phoenix

Continue uncovering Phoenix starting at Heritage and Science Park, packed with historical exhibits on the city's origins. Then marvel at the Martian-like scenery of Hole in the Rock before grabbing lunch with a view. Next up is the renowned Phoenix Zoo and its 5,000 animals from around the world. Kids will love spotting all their favorite species. If time allows, take a guided tour for insights into the zoo's conservation efforts. Wrap up downtown bar-hopping and sampling chef-driven fare at Phoenix's top restaurants.

Day 3 - Phoenix to Sedona:

Spend the day road-tripping up to stunning Sedona, stopping at scenic viewpoints along the way. In Sedona, cool off sliding down natural waterslides at Slide Rock State Park. Marvel at the area's famed red rocks at Bell Rock. Drive the iconic Upper Red Rock Loop Road, browsing artsy shops and restaurants. Spend the evening immersed in Sedona's lively nightlife scene.

Day 4 - Grand Canyon:

Rise early and drive to the awe-inspiring Grand Canyon. Take a narrated canyon rim tour by vehicle for sweeping views without the hiking. Descend into the canyon on foot to experience its immensity up close on a trail or two. Cap off the day browsing Tusayan's shops for souvenirs and treats before heading back.

Day 5 - Grand Canyon to Tucson:

Start the scenic drive back to Tucson, stopping at breathtaking viewpoints along the way. In Tucson, step back in time at the restored 20th-century Arizona-Sonora Desert Museum hotel. Wander through their artifacts chronicling Tucson and Sonora's past. At sunset, unwind amid nature at Fort Lowell Park's ponds and trails. End the night reveling in Tucson's lively music scene.

Day 6 - Tucson to Phoenix:

Make the shorter drive back to Phoenix, soaking up more of Arizona's stunning vistas en route. In Phoenix, revisit favorite attractions or experience new museums and viewpoints. Go shopping for trendy hiking gear before your flight home. Relax and reminisce on an unforgettable Arizona adventure!

This itinerary hits the highlights for a sweeping overview of Arizona's top sights. By road-tripping to its famous cities and natural wonders, you'll see why travelers return to Arizona again and again.

Travel
Jornal Section

Date of Visit: _____ **Days Spent:** _____

Weather Conditions	What I Visited

What I Bought

_____
_____
_____

Where I Slept

_____
_____
_____

Where I Ate	Who I Met

SECTION TO MARK THE SCORE FROM 0 TO 10

0   1   2   3   4   5   6   7   8   9   10

Beautiful Memory

_____
_____

JOURNAL LOG

Travel
Jornal Section

Date of Visit: **Days Spent:**

Weather Conditions	What I Visited

What I Bought	Where I Slept

Where I Ate	Who I Met

SECTION TO MARK THE SCORE FROM 0 TO 10

0   1   2   3   4   5   6   7   8   9   10

Beautiful Memory

JOURNAL LOG

Travel
Jornal Section

Date of Visit: **Days Spent:**

Weather Conditions

What I Visited

What I Bought

Where I Slept

Where I Ate

Who I Met

SECTION TO MARK THE SCORE FROM 0 TO 10

0　1　2　3　4　5　6　7　8　9　10

Beautiful Memory

JOURNAL LOG

Travel
Jornal Section

Date of Visit:

Days Spent:

Weather Conditions

What I Visited

What I Bought

Where I Slept

Where I Ate

Who I Met

SECTION TO MARK THE SCORE FROM 0 TO 10

0   1   2   3   4   5   6   7   8   9   10

Beautiful Memory

JOURNAL LOG

Travel
Jornal Section

Date of Visit: _____   **Days Spent:** _____

Weather Conditions

What I Visited

What I Bought

Where I Slept

Where I Ate

Who I Met

SECTION TO MARK THE SCORE FROM 0 TO 10

0   1   2   3   4   5   6   7   8   9   10

Beautiful Memory

JOURNAL LOG

Gete Your Bonus!

Get Your Bonus!

Absolutely loved your Arizona Bucket List Guide?

Help others make the most of their vacation by considering leaving a review!

Sharing your experience doesn't just take a few minutes, but also plays a crucial role in helping travelers choose the perfect guide.

Your insights will help them plan their dream holiday, avoiding the duds and making sure they hit all the must-see spots. Your review can make all the difference to someone else's vacation!

Go to the orders section of your Amazon profile and give your contribution if this guide is worth it for you!

Made in the USA
Las Vegas, NV
22 December 2023

83463724R00068